Solo Out Of Law School
A "*How Can*" Guide to Starting a Law Firm
as a New Attorney

Michael F. Brennan

Copyright © 2016 by Virtualis LLC

First Printing: 2016

ISBN 978-0-9974917-0-8

Virtualis LLC
17495 W. Bluff Drive
Grayslake, IL 60030

www.virtualis.us

Ordering Information:

Special discounts are available on quantity purchases by corporations, associations, educators, and others. For details, contact the publisher at the above listed address.

U.S. trade bookstores and wholesalers: Please contact Virtualis LLC Tel: (414) 982-5295 Fax: (414) 751-1397 or email contact.us@thevirtualattorney.com

Dedication

To my beautiful wife, Emilie and my friends, family and lifelong supporters.

Thank you. Your support and patience allows me to achieve my dreams.

Contents

Acknowledgements

First are foremost, I would like to thank my wife, Emilie for her years of dealing with my wild ideas. Em, your constant encouragement and never-wavering support has been the main reason that I've been able to live the life of my dreams. Starting a practice without you standing next to me would be utterly impossible. From day one, you have been my biggest cheerleader. You've been the voice of reason whenever things have gotten tough. Your eternal optimism has fueled me throughout this entire journey. I couldn't ask for a better teammate in life.

Thanks to my parents, Al and Cindy. You two have stood by me no matter where life has taken me. Whether it's been talking some sense into me during a middle-of-the-night phone call or a simple, "I'm proud of you," your love and support has given me the courage to make my life what I want to be.

To my siblings, Jane, Pat, Mary, and Joe, thanks for always supporting me. I know I'm not the most agreeable brother at times, but I've always been able to count on your encouragement.

Thanks to all my friends and legal colleagues. Your encouragement and support have always fueled my desire to become a better attorney.

Preface

Law school may teach you how to be a lawyer, but it falls painfully short when it comes to teaching the business of law. There are plenty of great books out there about the logistics of actually opening up a law firm, and I'd encourage you to check a few of them out because they can be tremendous resources as you launch your new practice.

But, let's get one thing cleared up off the bat: this is not one of those books.

This is not a "*how-to*" book about starting a law firm. It doesn't have any checklists or product reviews. It won't give you step-by-step instructions on how to hang out your shingle. If that's what you're looking for, then this book isn't for you.

I set out to write this book to present a different perspective on how to navigate the journey of starting a law firm. With a little searching, you can find plenty of information on trust accounts and how to conduct a client interview. Lists of the top ten ways to market your firm are more common than delays at airport security checkpoints. But for me, one thing was always impossible to find. That was lawyers willing to speak openly about the psychological challenges that come with hanging out a shingle.

It's not easy to take a subjective assessment of yourself in a way that allows you to articulate your fears, hopes, goals, and weaknesses. But, doing so enables you to face them in an objective way. And, to me, that was essential to my growth as a solo attorney.

This book is about principles. It's about mindset, motivation and viewing your work as a lawyer as something for which you can be proud.

It's not a "*how to*" guide to starting a law practice, it's a "*how can*" guide to starting a practice.   You may not agree with, or even relate to, everything I have to say in these pages, But, by reading about some of the things that I struggled with, it's my hope that you'll realize you're not alone.

You'll quickly realize that there is no right or wrong way to build your business. It's simply a matter of doing what works for you. My hope is that, by reading about what worked for me, the cogs in your head will begin to churn and inspire you to find the strength and creativity you need to keep pushing and keep building your firm into exactly what you want it to be.

With enough trial and error, it's relatively easy to master the logistics of operating a solo practice. Keeping the right mindset when you begin to tackle them is the hard part. This book is about the principles I followed to do it.

Introduction

2010 generally marks a low point for law school graduates in the United States. Still feeling the effects of the Great Recession and faced with a record number of new grads, law firms and corporate legal departments simply were not in a position to satisfy the plethora newly minted attorneys looking to begin their legal careers. In fact, beginning in 2007—generally considered the beginning of the Great Recession—the employment rate for new law graduates saw a decline from previously promising employment statistics. That decline continued for six straight years.[1] According to the National Association for Law Placement between 2007 and 2015, the employment rate for new law graduates decreased a total of 7.4 % from its high point of 91.9% in 2007.[2]

During the same period, at least two other major developments led to a change in the way recent law graduates and current students viewed the viability of beginning a solo practice. Developments in legal technology rapidly advanced while a fundamental shift from a seller's market— where firms were able to dictate the strategies and methods from delivery of legal services—to a buyer's market in which consumers were able to demand more custom-tailored legal solutions began to take shape. Technology made starting a new law practice with limited capital easier than ever before while the shift in legal service consumer mentalities created opportunities for client acquisition. Not only did starting a law practice become more conceivable for newly-minted JDs, it became a realistic and reasonable career move given market conditions.

Until recently, small firms were constrained in their operations by the limitations of legal technology solutions available in the market. But, changes in the way data is stored and accessed have dramatically expanded the array of practice management tools available to legal practitioners. Increases in cloud security and storage availability coupled with the relatively new convenience of being able to access the internet from anywhere with a cellular connection, through tablets and smartphones, have created a world where attorneys can forego some costs which previously were essential to operating a law firm.

Gone are the days when a physical office space and physical data servers were prerequisites to hanging out a shingle. Now, a new solo attorney can begin to grow a practice without much more than a smartphone, email, and a Dropbox account.

Technology has not only made it easier for lawyers to operate, but it has also had a profound effect on the way consumers of legal services assess their needs and primary objectives when retaining legal counsel.

Increased competition in the legal industry—from disruptive companies like UpCounsel, Avvo, and Shake—coupled with more accessible small firms has led consumers to demand responsiveness to their unique needs. Flexible billing structures, non-traditional representation models, and increased scalability have created a marketplace where consumers know what they want. This new marketplace has space for new players willing to tailor their marketing and representation models to highlight those desired value-adds.[3]

Quite simply, that reality has created a space in which new solos and small firms have an opportunity to carve out a share of the market—one previously dominated by larger firms.

It should come as no surprise then, that this new reality has led masses of recent law graduates, as well as current students, to consider solo practice as a viable career option. In the NALP's 2014 survey of 2013 law graduates, a very respectful 4.7% of new graduates reported being employed in a solo practice, though that number marks a far cry from the 5.7% of newly-minted attorneys practicing solo in 2010. However, it's noteworthy that the 2010 number was the highest it has been since 1997.

Even in a relatively ideal market for new competition to emerge in an already crowded legal services industry, for new attorneys brave enough to take the plunge, there is no shortage of challenges.

Perhaps most challenging amongst them is the ability to master the psychological challenges that are inherent in operating a law practice. Mental toughness and endurance are imperative to the sustained success of any solo practitioner. This book aims to give one young lawyer's perspective on how to keep your head in the game and give yourself a chance to make it.

Part 1: Plan the Attack

"It does not do to leave a live dragon out of your calculations, if you live near him."

— J.R.R. Tolkien

Tune Out the Negative Speak

If you're reading this book, then you are probably thinking about starting a law firm. Congratulations on even getting to this point of consideration! That alone is a huge step towards the metaphoric ledge from which you are thinking about inevitably leaping.

Let's get one thing out of the way right from the beginning: There is never a good time to start a law firm. Life has a funny way of creating all sorts of excuses that make it easy for us continually to put things off until the very inspiration we had to start something new—perhaps even revolutionary—fizzles away like a teapot losing steam.

It's human nature to doubt ourselves, our skills, and our abilities to succeed. For you, that could be a fear of not being able to support your two young children, or maybe it's a worry that your friends will look at your decision to strike out on your own as an indication that you were not "good enough" to get one of those plush Big Law jobs.

Here's what you need to remember: If everyone thought that going to law school, spending tens (if not hundreds) of thousands of dollars on education, and spending countless hours with your head buried in books and outlines just to say "no thanks" to becoming a big-shot lawyer sounded smart, they would be doing it. If everyone thought what you are about to consider doing was an excellent idea, then they would be doing it themselves.

People are going to doubt you. People are going to critique your decision to open up your own shop, and they are going to let you know about it. To be honest, one of those doubters from time to time is going to be you.

A harsh reality? Yes. One that you can weather? Absolutely. Being in business for yourself means that you are going to need to have incredibly thick skin. You're going to need to let things roll off your back, because at the end of the day, no one's views matter except for yours. People are going to judge you regardless of what you do, so it's best to accept that and forget about it.

You are no doubt reading this book for a reason. Whether you're passionate about a growing niche area of law, you think that billing 2200 hours a year at a large firm sounds like the easiest way to drive yourself to an early grave, or you just can't find work anywhere else, you've no doubt had at least a passing thought that starting your own firm may be your best chance at happiness and prosperity. You may have ideas on how to make the law more accessible to clients or more responsive to industry needs. You probably want to do things cheaper, faster, or more efficient than the established law firms that are already out there.

If everyone shared that same belief, they would be doing it too.

If you can't convince yourself that your reasons for wanting to start a law firm are valid, then you have set yourself up for failure before even getting started.

So, forget what other people think and stop worrying about what they may be saying. Most importantly, turn off that little voice in your head telling you that you can't do it and that you're going to fail. If you can't have confidence in yourself, you are destined to fail. You might as well realize that now because you are going to be your biggest cheerleader for the foreseeable future, so get on your good side now before things get tougher.

Think about why you want to start a law firm in the first place. Whether it's the freedom to work with the clients you want or the ability to make it to all of your daughter's soccer games, put that thought in the front of your mind and keep it there. Positive inspiration becomes your best friend when the road gets bumpy.

Turn Downsides Upside Down

Ꞩ∃ɒɩꙅ𝗇𝗐Ꝋꓷ

There are endless reasons not to start a law firm. Think about it.

After all, you have no experience, no paying clients, stiff competition from alternative legal service providers with massive marketing budgets and worst of all, a very real fear that people may actually know that you feel like you don't have the slightest clue what you are doing.

Most people would be hard-pressed to name another profession where an otherwise bright individual (you did make it through law school, sit for and pass the bar exam, after all) would look at the current state of his or her industry, see the bleak outlook, and move forward anyways.

So how are you going to use those challenges to your benefit?

As an attorney, you have acquired the ability to think about practically anything from multiple perspectives. In the field of law, two sides can look at the same set of accepted facts and draw two entirely different conclusions based on perspective. I'm a big fan of the television show, Dateline. Dateline has become mostly an investigative and true crime show typically showcasing hour long real life murder mysteries. One of the most frequent themes seen during an episode is police officers confronting a suspected killer (usually an ex-lover or spouse) with news that their loved one has been murdered. Often, the reaction by the unsuspecting interviewee is central to the question of guilt at a subsequent trial. Prosecutors and police very often point to subdued reactions as an indicator of guilt, the logic being that anyone who finds out that someone they care about has been killed will react in an outburst of forlorn emotion. Of course, those that react with such raucousness are also pinned as murders who must just be "putting on an act." Meanwhile, the defense views such reactions very differently. Perhaps the lover was so overcome with shock that the surreal news produced no emotional response. Or, naturally, for those that do react with an outburst of tears and desperate screams are reacting as one should react to hearing such life-altering news.

The point is that the undeniable facts of the situation can be interpreted in two entirely different ways depending on the lens through which they are viewed. As an attorney, you can probably see both sides of that coin. After all, it's your job to take the facts of any situation and use them to your client's advantage.

The ability to take that skill and apply it to building your business is going to be essential to your success. Just like a good prosecutor or defense attorney faced with a client's taped reaction in a murder investigation, you need to take the facts of your situation—whether real or perceived—and make them work to your benefit.

For example, maybe you're afraid that a potential client, when facing a choice between you—a newly minted attorney without much more than some mock trial experience and a summer internship at the District Attorney's office under your belt—and Joe Lawyer—who has practiced civil litigation for 25 years and successfully negotiated dozens of cases to six and seven-figure settlements—would never realistically chose you over him. But, that lack of experience does not have to be a negative. Instead, maybe it can mean that, unlike Mr. Lawyer, you have no preconceived notions of what the process should be. A settlement may not be in your client's best interests. Mr. Lawyer may know that he can take a quick paycheck by getting out early because he has handled a similar case before. To him, it's an open and close case.

Meanwhile, because of your lack of experience handling that type of case, you know that you are going to have to spend countless hours poring over statutes and case law to build a working knowledge of the issues involved. During your research, say that you find a rarely seen exception to the law that means your client will easily win on the merits if the case goes to trial, meaning a much higher payout for both you and your client.

The very lack of experience that you were viewing as a negative has all of a sudden turned into one of your strongest traits. Not knowing the law led you to uncover a way for your client to win big. It led you to see the case as a unique set of facts and circumstances while custom fitting a solution to those facts and circumstances.

Your lack of experience isn't a weakness. It's a strength. It enables you to represent clients without any preconceived notions of process or outcome.

What about the lack of paying clients? Clearly, your business is doomed to fail if you don't have a steady flow of new business coming in. And, in the beginning, taking on a new client is probably going to feel less probable than winning the lottery. Trust me, I've been there, and it gets better in a hurry. But until it does cash flow will be limited for a time as you get yourself established.

Unfortunate? Sure. But, look at it through a different lens. Without much technical legal work to do, you have ample time to focus on business development. You have the ability to spend your valuable and limited time perfecting your product and your delivery. What makes you stand out from the crowd? What's your angle? Akin to developing a prototype of a new invention, which can be tested and tweaked until it is the best it can be and ready for sale, you are going to need time to test and perfect your product. Honing what you have to offer future clients will give you the foundation you are going to need to survive long-term.

It's not a negative, it's a positive.

Lack of paying clients merely frees your schedule so that you can focus on developing a product that paying clients will want to use and recommend.

What about the lack of a steady stream of income? While it obviously may seem bad, try looking at it differently. Right now your funds are limited which means that you're going to need to maximize every dollar you spend, whether on advertising, software, networking or even paying for your personal needs. You simply don't have the luxury of wasting a single cent. That's going to force you to think about what expenses are essential to the operation of your firm. It's going to force you to cut out everything that is unnecessary to running a successful business.

Lack of money enables you to stay lean and able to adapt to changing market conditions.

What about all that competition? After all, you're not the only one out there practicing in your area of legal specialty. Stiff competition in a crowded industry may mean fighting harder for each client. But, it also means that there are countless other lawyers and firms from which to learn. Look at the firms that have been around for 100 years. What do they do that is so effective? What about the lawyers that have weathered the storm and figured out how to make it five or ten years on their own? How did they find their footing and how do they distinguish themselves from the masses? There is competition in every industry. Embrace it and make it work for you.

Lack of a client base, lack of income, and stiff competition can all potentially unhinge your fragile business before it gets off the ground by stomping you down mentally. But, viewed through a different lens, they can create an ideal environment in which to build a new business. It's all about perspective, and by turning negatives into positives, you are going to give yourself and your business more than a fighting chance to succeed.

Be Reasonable

There's nothing wrong with making plans for your business. You should consider all of the standards—cash flow, startup costs, when you are going to get clients, how you are going to get them, what you are going to do to generate referrals, and so on. But, my advice is that you need to be reasonable in your projections and your predictions.

The reality is that it's likely going to take much longer than you think to get to where you want to be.

When I started my business, I made the mistake of spending a substantial amount of my startup capital on advertising. I thought, almost embarrassingly, that if I pumped enough money into sponsored listings with search engines and social media websites, clients would be flocking to me right away. That certainly was not the case. Because of that hasty decision-making and unreasonable expectation, I put myself and my business into a hole early on. It would have been much easier, and much less stressful, to start slow and start smart.

It's easy to fall into a trap like I did, as we tend to tell ourselves something is bound to happen if we really want it. Silly, I know, but everyone can relate. It's human nature to have faith in our beliefs even if that faith is unfounded. By putting some reason behind those beliefs we can give faith an objective ally.

In the beginning, there is really very little that you need to get started. Any new attorney can send out a nice letter to family and friends letting them all know what he or she is doing. In fact, I guarantee that, if it hasn't happened already, your family and friends are going to be approaching you with plenty of legal issues they need advice about. Naturally, you're not going to be able to help everyone because you simply don't have the expertise. But my point is this: There will be work that you will be able to do, and it will come to you with little or no effort. Of course, it's probably not going to be enough to keep you up and running for the next few years, but it will hopefully show you that there are going to be people that need your help, and if you can keep reasonable expectations of how often those opportunities are going to arise, you are going to be ready to assist when they do.

That definitely does not mean that you shouldn't have lofty goals for what you want your business to become, but it does mean that you need to remember that it's going to take some time to reach those goals. In the short term, you need to look for small victories. Setting yourself up to meet realistic expectations is going to give you perspective and it's going to enable you to set realistic benchmarks for success. Hitting those will provide you with the motivation to keep pushing and give you optimism that you're on the right track. If you don't set reasonable expectations, you're never going to hit those benchmarks on time, and you may quickly convince yourself that you must be doing something wrong, or it's just not for you.

Set your expectations low and set yourself up for success.

Thinking that you're going to be pulling in $15,000 a month on a steady basis isn't realistic unless you are in an incredibly unique position in the market or geographically. I didn't pay myself a salary for six months as I built up a cash reserve and kept the lid on my spending. When I finally did pay myself, it was much less than my business plan or projections said it was going to be.

If you're expecting a $100,000 salary in your first year, don't bother taking the plunge into the world of solo practice. As has been said by practically any attorney who has done this before you, starting a firm isn't easy. And, a hefty paycheck certainly isn't going to come overnight. Reign in your expectations. Figure out the minimum you need to live and aim for that in the beginning. Your goal at the start is just to make it one more day. You're going to need time to feel out the market, establish yourself, and build your brand.

Understandably, it's hard to gauge where your firm will be in the future and when it will be there, so my advice is talk to other lawyers that have done it and ask them how long it was before they really truly were where they wanted to be. The answers might surprise you. They might give you a pessimistic view of whether you can actually succeed. But you know what? You can and you will, but only if you take it one day at a time and set reasonable expectations.

Oxford dictionary defines success as "the accomplishment of an aim or purpose." Often times we think of success in terms of achieving a particular level of wealth or outcome in a relationship or career. But look at the definition. Success is a finite concept. Once you find it, there's nowhere to go. You've hit the finish line. In business, how are you going to even begin to define what that finish line will be? Take a look at successful companies and you'll realize that they never hit the finish line—they aren't *successful*, but instead they are continually *reaching for success* while constantly redefining what success means to their businesses. You need to do the same thing.

Success by definition is a terminus. It's essential to the growth of your business that you don't ever feel satisfied. You should continually strive for success, but in doing so you need to always adjust your expectations and objectives in a way that is going to keep you moving forward. In business, there is no finish line.

Have a Plan B

Tradition says that entrepreneurs cannot, and should not think about failure—that it's not an option. But, just because it's not an *ideal* option doesn't mean it's not a very real possibility. To the contrary, I think common sense dictates that an entrepreneur needs to consider failure as an option. Time will tell how real of a possibility it may be, but ignoring the possibility that you just may not make it as a solo is a recipe for disaster.

I won't sugar coat it. Starting your own business means giving up a lot. Whether it's the cushy big-law job or the opportunity to join a boutique firm with a close-knit group of experienced attorneys, there are plenty of other ways you can use your legal skills to generate a paycheck.

And, it's not just law firm jobs you'll be passing up. Your law degree is an asset, and it makes you valuable. Even at a time when record numbers of attorneys are graduating from law school, you still possess something that can open plenty of doors for you. It takes courage to decide that you are not going to walk through any of those doors. There are plenty of voices out there that will tell you that, once you make that decision, you cannot and should not look back. "It's a choice you've made," they'll say, "so you need to live with it." And, doing so means that you probably missed out on other opportunities that may have otherwise been available to you.

I've never understood that logic. There are very few opportunities that simply pass you by. Why some people insist that you can't try to make it as a solo without giving up the option to later go work for a firm is beyond me. If things don't work out, you are still going to have the knowledge that you've gained through years of school, and likely now also years of experience practicing law. So, unless you've chosen to turn down your dream job to start your own law firm, my advice is to tune out those that will insist that your choice to go solo has doomed you to a lifetime of career failure if things do not work out.

On that note, I will say this: No one goes into anything expecting to fail. Otherwise, what's the point of trying it the first place? Setting out on a path with an expectation that you will never reach the end of the trail is foolish. But there's a difference between setting out on a course expecting to fail and thinking about what failure would mean.

Setting yourself up for failure is not an option, but thinking about the possibility is a necessity.

Think about failure. Picture the worst case scenario. What would things look like if you needed to admit that you didn't succeed as a solo attorney? Will your family leave you? Will you go broke with no hope of recovery, dooming yourself to life on the streets? Will your friends disown you because they can't imagine being surrounded by your negative energy? No, no, and no.

By thinking about failure and what it means for yourself and your life, you'll realize that it's not the end of the world. You can always stop, turn around, and go through the doors you may have passed up at the beginning of this journey you're about to embark on. The opportunities in the future may not be the same, but they will be just as attractive.

So, it's OK to think about what may happen. It's OK to think about what you may want to do if you come to a point where you decide you no longer have a desire to put any more time or effort into building your business.

Have a plan B. If your business works out (and I hope it does) then you will have done something that so few knowledgeable and creative attorneys have been able to figure out. But, for whatever reason, if it doesn't work out, you can hold your head high knowing that you gave it all you had. It does not mean that your legal career is over. It just means that you are making a decision to take it in another direction.

Keeping that perspective frees you up to enjoy the journey, no matter where it takes you.

Find Your Story

When people ask you why you started your own firm, what will you say?

Every year, thousands of people start their own businesses across the country. Whether it's because of a dead-end job that was no longer tolerable or because a little lightbulb went off with the next great idea that the world was missing out on, everyone's journey to being self-employed is a different one.

The son of a coffee roaster, Alfred Peet grew up in the Netherlands with an appreciation for quality coffee. However, upon moving to the United States after World War II, Peet quickly found the coffee culture much different. Coffee across Europe was something to be appreciated, while in America, quite the opposite was true. In the Land of the Free, coffee was something to be drunk and not thought about (and as many would say, for good reason too. In fact, Peet himself famously referred to it as, "the lousiest coffee in the world"). Seeking to introduce a more European appreciation for coffee drinking to the community, Peet opened a small coffee shop in Berkeley, California where he roasted his own coffee beans using techniques from his homeland. He focused on using quality beans and slow, deliberate roasting. Peet's appreciation of quality led to more than just a good cup of joe. It created an experience. His tiny Berkeley shop became a favorite hangout for the nonconformist contingent of Berkeley residents as they were seemingly attracted to this new anti-establishment café.

Peet's vision for what coffee should be quickly spread outside of Berkeley. In fact, Gordon Bowker, Jerry Baldwin and Zev Siegl were so interested in Peet's new brew that they eagerly learned his methods and opened their own coffee shop in Seattle (yes, that one).

Today, there are over 200 Peet's locations nationwide, Starbucks on practically every corner, and countless smalltime operations across the country that are based on Peet's idea of what the coffee drinking experience should be.

David McConnell initially worked as a travelling door-to-door book salesman, who, like many travelling salesmen, was astutely aware of his audience's desire (or lack thereof) for his product. Looking for a way to stick around houses long enough to at least be able to pitch his product, McConnell began offering free samples of homemade perfume that he blended himself to housewives in exchange for the opportunity to talk about his books. He quickly realized that the women were far more interested in the scents than the books. Thus, he quit peddling books and started the California Perfume Company, today known as Avon. McConnell borrowed the same concepts from his days selling books door-to-door and applied them to the sale of cosmetics.[4] Today, Avon has over 6 million representatives and totals more than $8 billion in sales worldwide. [5]

Everyone's story is unique. Alfred Peet did not set out to start a coffee revolution in the United States. He just wanted some good coffee. David McConnell just hated selling books and kept his eyes open for new opportunities. The point is that you have gotten to this stage in life through an intricate web of random and not-so-random decisions, events, and inspirations. They form you into the person that you are and your outlook on the world. No one else has your perspective or your unique desire for what you want the future to be.

So, figure out what drives you and how you can use that inspiration to do something unique. Draw on it to set yourself apart from the thousands of other lawyers and law firms that make up your competition, and use it to build something the world has yet to see.

Find your story and 30 years from now maybe you'll be the next Alfred Peet.

Get Your Head Right

It should go without saying that starting your own business requires some preparation. You would not run a marathon without properly training for months, and starting a business is no different.

That's not to say that you need to spend months thinking about how every little detail is going to work because chances are almost certain that things are not going to go exactly according to your plan. The growth cycle of a small business and its ultimate fate is simply too speculative for you to be able to approach it with any level of certainty. But, you do still need to prepare yourself for the journey ahead.

Being a small-business owner, or more specifically the owner of your own law firm, is going to test your resolve. There are going to be days that you are going to wake up and say, "What the hell am I doing?" You are going to doubt yourself and you are going to question your decision to tread out on your own path. But, do you know what? That is completely normal.

An inquiry through any search engine will reveal the bleak statistics on the failure rate of new businesses. It's far too easy to look at those statistics and wonder why you and your new firm will be any different. Asking yourself how you are going to succeed when so many of those that have come before you just couldn't cut it is OK.

It's OK to think about what the future may inevitably hold for your firm.

So the question, then, is what separates the "*haves*" from the "*have nots?*" There are probably dozens of ways to answer that question, and depending on who you ask, you will likely get a number of varying responses. Lack of planning, poor management, insufficient capital, lack of focus, and a handful of other reasons are all commonly cited as reasons why new businesses fail. But, to me what separates the "*haves*" from the "*have nots*" is not a desire to succeed, because every entrepreneur has got that. Rather, it's the ability to keep going when doubt creeps in. It's mental toughness. Mental toughness gives you an edge. It allows you to keep yourself invested in your business regardless of the challenges it may come up against. It gives you the ability to find solutions to those other commonly listed reasons why businesses fail.

Running a marathon is traditionally viewed as one of the greatest feats of physical activity. While average fitness buffs can cover the 26.2 miles in around three-and-a-half hours, elite professional marathoners can flirt with times around two hours. That averages out to a cool 4:58 per mile. For even the most regular of amateur runners, that sub-five minute per mile pace is unfathomable. So what does it take to accomplish such an immense feat? American marathon record-holder Khalid Khannouchi[6] offered the following insight to USA today:

> "It's a combination of discipline, hard work, harshness of weather. The most difficult part is keeping your focus for a long period of time. The time I like to prepare for a marathon is four months. Marathoners seem either to be training or getting ready for the next workout. You wake up every morning and you know what you have to do. You have long mileage to accumulate. Sometimes you're already tired from your last two or three workouts. You still have to wake up, have the motivation and go outside and do the training.

The key is you have to be patient mentally and physically. Control of emotions is important. I've found a lot of people can't do that, even if they are professionals. You have to run smart. Sometimes I run in the back of the (lead) group, five to 10 seconds behind. I'm pacing myself and body the way that suits me to run better. That's difficult to do sometimes." [7]

Building a law practice is just like running a marathon. And, like a marathon runner, you need to prepare mentally for the race ahead. It takes a combination of discipline, hard work, and tremendous focus. It requires you to push forward even when you've been drained of all motivation. You need to realize that, at times, you're going to doubt yourself. Whether it's your strategy for finding clients or your interpretation of a particular law, you're going to question your decisions. It's simply human nature to do so.

So, get ready to doubt yourself and have a plan for how you'll tackle that.

Having an awareness that you're inevitably going to have days where you question your decisions will prepare you to identify the negative self-talk and re-characterize it when those days come.

It's important to realize that setbacks aren't a reflection of you. Make them impersonal, temporary and precise, and just like Khannouchi when he's training for a marathon, get out there and keep pushing.

There are going to be days when the race seems so incredibly long, when the steps to success seem infinitely large. It's essential to develop an ability to look at the big picture so that you are able to realize that, while you may not be near the end of your journey of building a successful business, you have taken measurable strides to keep moving forward. Without that, you'll doom yourself to failure.

When asked his secrets to success as a runner, Khannouchi said:

"You always set a goal, but you can't have too high an expectation. If you know you can run 3 hours or 3:30, don't think about 2 hours 40. You can think about that in four, five years if you stay healthy."

Like a marathon runner setting a realistic goal for finishing time, a new attorney needs to develop a plan that will propel her towards a realistic goal. A lot of that comes from being honest with yourself about what you are capable of.

As Khannouchi said, you can always think about doing something bigger, better and bolder. But, keeping perspective on where you need to go and what you can realistically reach are essential to maintaining the mindset you need to succeed.

The "F Word"

No book about starting a business would be complete without touching on the issue of funding. Where should you get it? How much do you need? What should you be using it for? Valid and significant questions, all. But with that said, you can find ideas on what to do and not do in plenty of other places. As you've gathered by now, this isn't a step-by-step guide about how to build your company.

I will say this. Unless you're in a unique situation—like you won the lottery and are just starting your own firm so you don't get bored of your millionaire lifestyle—you will need to make sacrifices financially. Figure out the bare minimum you need to get by, and ask yourself, "If that was all I was able to afford, would I be OK?" Be honest with yourself. Do you really need that new jersey of your favorite NFL player every fall? Are you OK with a romantic night out at Taco Bell with your spouse instead of the new swanky gastropub? Decide what you need to stay afloat, at least for the foreseeable future, and forget the rest. Having an honest conversation with yourself about finances will allow you to do two things.

First, you'll have a financial benchmark that absolutely must be hit in order to fight another day. Really, that's all I'd tell you to focus on—your *bare-minimum benchmark*. Don't worry about every dollar and every expense. Maybe you spent more on web development costs than you had budgeted. Maybe you anticipated that your real estate practice would account for 40% of your revenue, but in reality it consistently ends up being only around 30% every month. I'm sure you can find plenty of number-junkies that would passionately disagree with my approach. But honestly, who cares? Who cares if each and every projection you make pans out? You're not a public company, you don't have shareholders to answer to, and you almost certainly are not backed by any sort of venture or angel funding.

No one cares about the intricate financial details of your new operation. All that's important is that you ended up hitting your bare-minimum benchmark. Because, at the end of the day, all that matters is that you managed to buy yourself one more week, or month, or quarter, or whatever arbitrary time period you're using to measure your success.

There will be plenty of time to analyze your income and expenses in order to really hone in on what makes your practice tick. But, in the beginning that's all irrelevant.

You are going to take a lot of the stress out of the financial worries that consume most small business owners if you can simplify the way you think about money. Once you are able to ignore (just initially) the details of your finances, you'll free yourself to focus on objectively building your business.

It's far too easy to obsess over every dollar, and by doing so, you're spending your energy focusing on an outcome. That means you're not focusing on the processes that can get you to the outcome. And, that will doom your business. So, figure out that bare-minimum benchmark and forget the rest for the time being.

The second thing that an honest contemplation about finances will give you is articulable expectations for your ultimate success as a solo. I highly doubt that you are only thinking about going solo for financial reasons. If you are, then it flat out isn't for you. If a large paycheck is the way you define success, then you are much better off working for an established firm with its corollary financial security.

I'm guessing that you're considering starting your own firm because you want something more. Maybe you want to start your own firm because it offers you the freedom to make your own schedule or the ability to represent a particular type of client. Maybe it's because you want to prove to yourself that you can do it. Or, maybe you just want the ability to attend your kid's soccer games without having to worry about picking up the slack while some partner in your firm spends time with his family instead.

Articulate what that "*more*" is for you. By doing so, you're going to redefine success. You won't be clinging to the thought that you're not successful if you don't make partner by 35, or that you're stuck in second chair in court far longer than some of your peers at other firms. Rather, you'll be focusing on the things that you find important and fulfilling instead of those which society says matter.

So, when those challenging months inevitably arise, when client numbers are down, and the income isn't what you had anticipated, you'll be able to step back and remember that you didn't start your business only for financial reasons. You started it for the "more."

Yes, of course finances are important. Having income is essential to being able to continue to do what you love. But, when the money isn't what you hoped it would be, falling back on the non-financial reasons you started your business will give you the strength and mental resolve to fight another day. That itself is a success.

Part 2: Get Started

"You can't build a reputation on what you are going to do."

— Henry Ford

Define Your Perfect Client

Close your eyes and imagine your ideal client. How old is she? What's her family situation? Does she have particular interests or hobbies? With whom does she associate? Does she speak a particular language? Belong to a certain group? Have a certain type of job? Fit into a defined socio-economic status? Where would she hang out? Does she interact with certain people? What shapes her values?

Write down everything you can imagine about that person. Be specific. Describe the traits that make her who she is.

Now, think about the hypothetical reason for which that ideal client wants to hire an attorney. What happened? Did she get injured? Wronged? If so, how and when did it happen?

Or maybe, that ideal client wasn't injured or wronged. Perhaps some life event led her to realize the importance of your services. Did she have a child? Was there a death in the family? Maybe she started a new business or she made the decision to retire after a long and fruitful career building a company and she needs you to lend your legal expertise to her exit plan.

Imagine the exact scenario in which that ideal client would come to realize that she needs legal representation—specifically the type of representation you offer.

Now, put yourself in that client's shoes and think about the kind of lawyer that she would want to hire. Where is his office? Does he always wear a suit and tie or is he more casual? Is he relatable? Responsive? What makes him seem trustworthy? Knowledgeable? Does age matter? What about demeanor? How does he communicate? Specifically, does he always meet in person or prefer email and phone conversations? How does he charge for his services- hourly, flat-fees, retainer-based representation, or contingent fees?

Write it down.

Look at the lawyer that you just described on that page. That is who you need to be to work with the ideal client you just described on the precise matters in which your passion resides.

More specifically, defining that perfect client will help you decide what your firm's image should be, where you should set up shop, and how much you should charge. It will tell you what groups you should belong to, influential people you should get to know, how to dress, how to talk, how to advertise, and how to carry yourself. It's going to influence the choices you make for your firm's colors, logo, motto, web layout, blog, sphere of influence and anything else that forms the persona of your company.

From my time building relationships with other solo attorneys— specifically young ones—it has become incredibly clear to me which ones understand the importance of defining their ideal client because those are the attorneys that are successful. I think it can be too tempting for a new attorney to take on representing any client that walks through the door. But, as you'll hear time and time again if you speak with other lawyers, those are the folks that have trouble sustaining a successful law practice. Because, while those clients may offer a quick paycheck, they offer absolutely nothing in the way of business development.

My practice focuses on two areas—estate planning and transactional business law for entrepreneurs and small businesses. It's a cloud-based virtual practice because I've found that busy young families and new business owners may not necessarily have the time to commit to office visits or lengthy in-person status meetings when they are carrying full-time jobs while balancing their family lives. The last thing any of them need is an additional time commitment. More so, I know that it's the overwhelming preference of many folks today to communicate via indirect methods like text and email, which enables them to respond on their timelines rather than in real time as is required when talking by phone or meeting in person.

From my internal business operations to the technology I use; from the way I market to the way I communicate, I've focused my entire practice on catering to my ideal clients. Could I take on a small claims collection matter from a retired widow? Sure. I think I could handle it. But, would that lead to more estate planning referrals for young millennial families? Almost certainly not. And, by taking on that collections case, not only would I be taking away from the finite time and resources I have to invest in developing my practice on my terms but I essentially would have watered down my product. If I can't be honest with myself about the kind of practice I'm running, then how can I possibly explain it to a client with a straight face? What message does it send to my referral sources if I say that I focus on estate planning for young millennial families when I just took on a case that couldn't be further from that? If I were in their shoes, it would make me second guess the cases I may be referring to myself.

If your perfect client is a college-educated, young thirty-something couple with two young children that owns their own home in the suburbs, has a net worth of around $500,000, and you practice estate planning, your firm's image is going to be different than if your ideal client is a divorcing mother whom you want to help retain custody of her two young children over an abusive ex-spouse.

Knowing who your ideal client is will enable you to determine what you can do to make sure that you present an appropriate image to potential clients. It's going to tell your colleagues and peers which potential client makes a great referral, and it's going to define you as a practitioner. It's going to help you develop your firm into something unique-something that stands out from the competition.

Forget the Bells and Whistles

SIMPLE.

If there is one thing that did not exist ten years ago which has changed the potential to find success starting a law firm above all else, it's access to a seemingly endless number of affordable tools that increase efficiency and enable a young lawyer to operate a business with minimal physical infrastructure. That accessibility has arisen primarily through the advent of cloud computing and cloud-based software and services.

Whether it's accounting software, credit card billing, practice management, online fax or phone services, video conferencing, data management, storage, or contact management, cloud services help make running a one-man or one-woman business possible. And, they make it possible when operating with a limited budget.

Finding the right mix of cloud solutions for your firm can help you create the infrastructure necessary to operate your practice in any manner you choose. Whether you want to create a purely virtual law firm or you're only looking for a technological solution to help keep yourself organized in the courtroom, cloud-based services can make you more effective and more efficient as a lawyer.

But with the increased functionality and accessibility that comes with incorporating cloud-based solutions into your practice comes a danger that has the potential to severely damage your new, and still very fragile, business. That is the temptation to overspend on innovative but entirely necessary technology.

Having a workable practice management suite is essential. Having a program that can keep your numbers straight is vital to knowing your bottom line, income, and expenses. If you find yourself in court frequently, there are a number of tools that can help you effectively present your case. But, it's important to draw a line somewhere.

Shortly after I started my practice, I remember developing an interest in a new cloud-based customer relationship management system geared specifically towards law firms. It would have enabled me to track interactions with clients, potential clients, and my referral network. For someone like me that notoriously can't remember what I had for lunch yesterday or where I parked my car when running into the store, it seemed like an ideal addition to my practice. But, at around $50 per month, I was hesitant to take on the commitment. After all, even though I had taken my own advice of focusing on a bare-minimum benchmark rather than a more detailed budgetary analysis, it was clear enough to me that even a $50 per month commitment was going to make a dent in my small expense budget.

After giving it some thought, I realized that with a little bit of discipline I could track the same important details that this particular CRM would monitor by manually plugging them into spreadsheets. Would it be more work? Of course. And, it certainly wouldn't be a sustainable practice when my firm (hopefully) grew, but for the time being, it was more than worth the $50 per month savings. So, I said no to the CRM subscription. While my spreadsheet method didn't have all the features the CRM tool had—like automated messaging—it did what I needed it to do. And, it did it for free.

It's easy to get caught in a trap of thinking that tools are going to bring success. You may think, "If only X were easier, I'd have more time to focus on finding clients." or, "If my clients could pay me with a credit card, then I wouldn't have to deal with late payments." But, that's usually not the case.

In reality, the only thing those extra bells and whistles are going to do is drain your bank account before you even have an opportunity to make those tools work for you.

In the beginning, forget the bells and whistles.

I promise that you are going to have all the time in the world to experiment with new tools and technology once you build a solid foundation for your business. But, in the beginning, you need to have one goal. That goal is to do quality work for paying clients. Managing your networking contacts and potential clients with a fancy SaaS solution is not going to just automatically lead to a referral-based, self-sustaining firm.

So, my advice for you is to set yourself up with the bare minimum required to do your job. For me, and I would guess for most attorneys, that includes:

- a computer
- a phone
- an email address
- a way to keep track of your money
- a way to keep track of your clients.

Everything else is extra. Remember that your clients are paying for your personality and expertise. It doesn't matter that clients can sign engagement letters electronically. What matters is that they want to sign those engagement letters with you in the first place.

Keep that perspective and there will quickly come a time to add all of the bells and whistles you want. Don't, and chances are good that your firm won't be around long enough to enjoy them anyways.

Build a Board of Directors

Making the choice to go solo does not have to mean going it alone. While you may be the only one on the front lines when it comes to making decisions about which clients to take, what legal tactics to employ and what advice to provide, as any successful CEO will tell you, having a trusted team of advisors will prove invaluable to growing your business.

Your board of directors does not need to be an actual formal advisory arm of your business. In fact, it shouldn't be. Rather, your board should be made up of trusted role models that can share advice on the trials and tribulations inherent in starting a business. They can be other lawyers, but they don't have to be.

Every young lawyer needs a network of more experienced attorneys that know the intricacies of practicing law. From a technical standpoint, other lawyers are your best sources of advice if you want to make sure you're taking care of your clients.

But, it's those that have earned their stripes in the corporate world that are going to be invaluable to the ultimate success of your business. They are going to be able to tell you what your financial figures say, why your marketing campaign isn't working, and how effectively your branding is directly correlating to the client base that you are hopefully building.

They are the ones that are going to open your eyes to market trends and keep you focused on non-legal goals and objectives.

When I started my business, I relied heavily on the advice of some tremendous voices in both the legal world as well as the purely corporate world. My father, a man who has spent his entire career in corporate America, became one of my most frequent sounding boards for everything from determining the appropriate financial analysis to use for an operation scaled at the level of my firm to identifying essential distribution channels for the niche services I was offering and how to maximize the return I saw on the time and resources I infused into those channels. He has absolutely no legal education or background, but for a political science major like me that had little interest in finance accounting or traditional theories of business management, his expertise proved to be essential to infusing my firm with life.

I also relied (and still do) on the advice and knowledge of other attorneys. From solos a few years my senior, to experienced practitioners that were in the twilight of their careers when I was just beginning mine, each was able to offer a unique perspective on the challenges that face lawyers and law firms, both big and small, in an ever-changing economy.

Whether it was advice to invoice in the middle of a month so that my bill fit into a client's budget for the following month or an analysis of efficient and effective ways to automate processes, those folks each gave me valuable insight into the ways I could make my business most effective.

My reliance on both lawyers and non-lawyers alike was, and continues to be, essential to the evolution and growth of my firm.

Whether it's the practice of law or the sale of car tires, businesses are all the same. It's only the product you're selling that's different.

Lawyers know how to practice law. Business people know how to build businesses. Both are essential to building a law firm that thrives. So, take advantage of their advice and take it often.

Whether it's family, friends in business, your pastor, your dentist, a mentor from the vast roles of other experienced attorneys willing to serve as mentors, connections from an entrepreneurial networking group, or anyone else that has a unique perspective, surround yourself with other people that can see your business through a various lenses. Diversifying the perspectives that others will provide is essential.

There are millions of successful business and legal minds out there. Learning even just a little about what makes them successful and putting those ideas to work in your own business is the best way to add yourself to their ranks.

Learn Everything You Can About Sales

"The good lawyer is the great salesman." – Janet Reno

Did you know that nearly 50% of all practicing lawyers in the United States are solo?[8] That may not come as a surprise given the state of the legal industry since the Great Recession. But, what is surprising is that, even when faced with such staggering statistics, law schools across the country are failing to teach their students the basics of running their own businesses.

While law schools may have clinical programs, internship opportunities, and artificial programs, like mock trial that present students with opportunities to learn the *practice of law*, it's a rare occurrence to find a school that is truly teaching the *business of law*. Important topics like marketing a firm, incorporating appropriate software and technology, hiring support staff, accounting, finance, general operations, and organizational structure are commonly overlooked.

Now, suggesting that teaching the business of law should be the primary concern of law schools is a ridiculous idea. After all, what good are business skills if the product that is being sold isn't up to snuff?

However, the natural consequence arising from the modern structure of legal education in the United States is that new attorneys have little working knowledge of the day-to-day operations that make a law firm work.

Associates at larger firms have the benefit of immersing themselves in the developed operations of established businesses. They can learn the ins and outs of business from more senior members of the firm. As a solo straight out of school, or even one that may have started at another firm for a few years before hanging out a shingle, you don't have that luxury.

You are now going to face the same challenges as any small business owner. Challenges that, for many, are hedged by the knowledge they gained from formal business studies or practical experience. From accounting to formulating a marketing plan; from customer service to product development, all of a sudden you are going to need to wear a dozen hats, and you are going to need to know how to wear them stylishly if you want to give yourself a chance to succeed.

Amongst the seemingly endless web of skills you are going to need to excel at, one always stands out above the rest. It's a skill that, if mastered, can practically guarantee your success.

Like many who start their own firms in the first few years after graduation from law school, I didn't take the plunge all at once. Instead, I got my feet wet and then slowly worked my way in from the shallow end. With bills to pay, I took a job working in-house at a large company drafting and negotiating commercial contracts. The relationship between the things I learned and the fields of law in which I hoped to practice— estate planning and entrepreneurial law—was tenuous, at best. Of course now I help plenty of clients draft and reviews contracts of various types, but aside from negotiating skills and the importance of proper legal semantics, I wasn't exactly building my skills in those other specialties.

That's not to say that the experience was fruitless. To the contrary, it gave me an appreciation for a skill that is essential for any attorney— especially a solo—to be successful.

I'm talking about sales.

In my position, I would commonly find myself managing a number of moving pieces independent of the actual negotiation of legal language. It was part of my unwritten job description to manage the relationships that circulated around those moving pieces—from customers and their attorneys to other in-house business leaders, and most memorably, the company's sales associates.

Boy, did those people knew how to sell. Every word each of them spoke had purpose and that purpose was to close the sale. Whether it was selling their product, or selling their position to me, they knew how to get what they wanted. At times, I would find myself nearly persuaded to change my position even if there was absolutely no logical reason to do so. Unlimited liability for us? "Well I guess that makes sense. After all, you have been working on this deal for two years and I'm the only thing standing between the company and a multi-million dollar sale." (For the record, I always found my way back to my responsibilities as a lawyer instead of giving in to the pressure to "let some things slide.").

But, by being surrounded by, and interacting with, those sales professionals on a daily basis, I picked up on subtle communication techniques that they used to convince me to buy into their positions without even realizing that I had.

Many of us become lawyers because it's an easy profession in which to blend in with the crowd, one in which you can keep your head down, do the work, and get paid. In large firms, where partners handle the majority of client interactions while young associates do the grunt work in back offices, that may be possible. But, going into solo practice means that if you aren't willing and able to effectively interact with potential clients—if you aren't able to convince people that they need what you have to offer—you're not going to last long.

When you start your own business, you'll quickly find that, whether you like it or not, your salesperson hat is going to be one you wear the most. Your entire livelihood is going to depend on your ability to sell what you have to your ideal client over and over again. That leaves you with no choice but to learn everything you can about how to effectively sell and how to do it consistently.

There are hundreds of books out there on the psychology of sales techniques. This obviously is not one of them, but I'd strongly encourage you to read a few and invest in developing your sales skills, because, if you're not able to sell yourself and your firm, your business is doomed to fail.

Pick Up Where the Last Guy Left Off

As Thomas Edison once stated, "*I start where the last man left off*."[9]

The key to building a successful business is having the ability to look at the way things are currently done and figure out a way to do them better.

Taxicabs have been a mainstay in global transportation for decades. With due respect for the rickshaw industry, the taxi industry—especially in Western countries—enjoyed a practical monopoly on private urban transportation until very recently. Most people, without so much of a second thought, would consider a cab the obvious choice for getting from point A to point B whether for a lunch meeting or a night out on the town. However, that doesn't mean it is without flaws. For anyone that has tried to grab a cab outside a busy bar at 1:00 AM on New Year's Day can understand the limits that a transportation structure based on being in the right place at the right time presents.

Enter, Travis Kalanick.

While on a trip to Paris for a tech conference, Kalanick and his friend, Garrett Camp had a hard time hailing a cab in the busy city. Faced with an all-too-common scenario, Kalanick and Camp came up with a simple idea: they would create a way to hail a cab with the push of a button.

That simple idea grew into Uber, the mega-popular on-demand chauffeur service.

Kalanick and Camp didn't set out to change the foundation of the cab industry. After all, being transported from one place to another by someone else is a concept as old as time. But, what they did set out to change was the way that concept was put into action. Taxi companies face a litany of challenges that hinder their efficiency. From state and local regulations to monopolization of operating licenses, there are numerous issues that prevent taxi companies from effectively serving the needs of their consumers.

By structuring a business built around independent contractors as drivers, Uber has been able to sidestep many of those hindrances.

A flex-based pricing model dictated by the simple dynamics of supply and demand ensures that there are a sufficient number of operators available to meet consumer needs, effectively ensuring that users will never again have to experience the far too common conundrum Kalanick and Garrett faces on that night in Paris back in 2008.

Travis Kalanick and Garrett Camp came up with an idea so simple on its face yet so monumental in its effect. To implement their vision, they found simple solutions to improve on incredibly common problems which, at some time or another, have been faced by anyone that has ever taken a ride in a cab. No cash? With Uber, you pay with a pre-programmed credit card which directly deducts your fare upon arrival at your destination. Trouble figuring out how much to tip your driver? Uber builds the tip into your fare. Trouble finding a cab? Uber lets you summon one to a specific address with the push of a button. Don't know exactly where you are? Good thing Uber is linked to GPS and can figure that out for you.

Like the taxicab industry, the practice of law is built on a simple premise. In law, that is the premise that one's knowledge of a complex web of information can be used to help those less educated reach a favorable outcome. While various methods have been developed to accomplish that objective throughout the years, lawyers are slow to change their ways to keep up with an ever-evolving world.

Like Kalanick and Camp did when they started Uber and caused the largest disruption the taxi industry has even seen, you have an opportunity to disrupt an industry rooted in history and routine simply by thinking about how to make it work better for the individuals it serves.

While you may look at your new law firm and see something that's been done thousands of times before, it's important to realize that you have something unique to offer to clients. You have something that they can't get at any old law firm. The key is to figure out what that something is.

Kalanick and Camp just wanted a better way to find a ride. For you, it may be just as simple.

It's All About Baby Steps

There's an annual race that takes place in the backcountry mountains of Tennessee called the Barkley Marathons. I use the term *race* loosely because it isn't much of a race at all in the traditional sense. In reality, the annual Appalachian event more closely resembles a reality television show fit for Discovery Channel. The Barkley Marathons are meant to break participants down, to see them fail and give in to the impossibility of succeeding at something so monumental that, in its nearly thirty-year history, the event has seen only fourteen finishers. Quite simply, it is designed to test the very threads of human willpower and survival.

That's because the race consists of a twenty-mile-long course that weaves up and down unmarked trails through some of the most mountainous and dense terrain in the continental United States. Participants must complete five loops, for a total traveled distance of 100 miles—an act seemingly so unreasonable and impossible that the addition of a sixty-hour time limit is certainly unnecessary. [10]

Given the monumental effort required for completion, it's no wonder that so few people have actually completed the race. In fact, even the most physically gifted and mentally fortuitous participants commonly give up after completing only one or two loops, and that's only if luck was on their side. While every participant dreams about finishing the race, even competing in the first place is something that many come to see as a victory in and of itself.

Our minds are wired to set lofty goals. Whether the objective is to complete the entirety of the Barkley Marathons or create a business that thrives and survives for a lifetime, it's human nature to aim for the result and find satisfaction only in its achievement.

Setting lofty goals and envisioning the ultimate result is no doubt something for which every business founder should strive. After all, I'd guess you're not setting out to start a law firm with the hope that you will be able to give it all up in three years. But, having an end goal goes hand in hand with setting benchmarks for success on the way to that ultimate objective.

In the first weeks of my new firm's existence I, like any other entrepreneur, questioned what the future held. Of course, there is no way to know what the future holds without setting out on the journey. We can always hope for a particular outcome or imagine our lives if everything played out perfectly, but there is no way to guarantee we will ever get there.

The weight of that reality can be so heavy that it paralyzes even the most optimistic go-getters. For introverted and somewhat pessimistic folks like me, it can be crippling without knowing how to face it. And, what I found is facing it meant redefining the journey.

In those early weeks of my practice, I did a lot of reading about success. I don't recall what it was or who wrote it, but at some point, I came across a line that resonated with me—one that changed my entire mentality towards building my business. I put it on a sticky note and attached it to the monitor on my desk. To this day I still read those words of wisdom every single morning:

> *"Building a great business is about thousands of baby steps all added up. But, you'll NEVER get to the end without the first few steps."*

For the participants in the Barkley Marathons, it's considered a success just to start the race. It's a success to complete one loop. Successfully completing the entire race depends on the completion of thousands of baby steps each building on the preceding step. For me, success is waking up every morning with the goal of moving my firm one step further away from the start line. For me, it's about advancing on the journey and asking myself, "What can I do today to make my firm better than it was yesterday?"

You need to approach your business the same way. Set goals for yourself that are attainable and are attainable often. Meeting those goals and completing those steps is not only going to give you the motivation to keep pushing forward towards your ultimate goal, but it's also going to give you articulated benchmarks to work towards that seems reachable.

Having a business that supports the lifestyle you imagine for yourself is a wonderful thing to shoot for. But, realize that you're going to lose your sanity and your drive to succeed if you don't find value in what you're doing to get there. Take it one step at a time and you'll be fine.

Forget About Being a Lawyer

As a solo attorney, you need to wear multiple hats: one for business-building, one for business-running, and one for "lawyering". Each of those roles plays a vital role in the success you will or will not ultimately have in growing your firm, but at times certain roles are more important than others. One of those times is during the initial stages of growth.

As a general rule, lawyers are a very detail-oriented bunch. When entering a profession where being good at your job can hinge on a single word in a contract or brief, that isn't surprising. What is surprising, at least to me, is that most lawyers have a hard time ever separating themselves from that hyper-detailed mentality. That's a problem when it comes to building a solo practice. As famed Irish playwright George Bernard Shaw once famously penned,

> *"You see things; and you say why?" But I dream things that never were; and I say why not?* "[11]

As far as I'm concerned, that might as well have been written about the difference between lawyers and entrepreneurs. The difference between most lawyers and successful entrepreneurs is the ability to look at a problem on a larger scale. You need to strive to be the "*I*" in that quote, not the "*You*."

The ability to micro-analyze a problem is an essential skill to having success as an attorney. But as a solo, that's not enough. Because, as a solo you are not only a lawyer, you're an entrepreneur. And, if you want to get your new firm up and running successfully, you need to flip a mental switch and think like an entrepreneur.

The primary objective in the early days of your firm's existence needs to be positioning your brand. By positioning your brand, I mean deciding where your firm will fit into the legal market. Think back to the exercise you did a few chapters ago when you defined your perfect client. Positioning your brand means successfully placing yourself in the legal market so that you can efficaciously target and acquire that potential client. That means that you need to step outside of the hyper-analytic world in which attorneys thrive and think about the bigger picture.

Far too many young lawyers focus far too much on the legal role of an attorney—the "lawyering," so to speak. The reason is obvious. Throughout law school, we are taught to read the law, analyze the facts, and formulate an argument that is most advantageous to our client. Very rarely are we asked to think about who the clients will be, where they will come from, how much we may charge them, or how we will interact with them in an initial consultation.

Your business is not going to go anywhere without putting some thought and effort into developing a client acquisition strategy, developing a brand, formulating a memorable identity and defining a target demographic. That requires putting on your business-building hat.

Is the "lawyering" part necessary? You better believe it. But, no one is even going to have an opportunity to see how good you may be at lawyering if you can't effectively position your firm in a way that successfully targets and acquires clients. Putting the work into developing an entrepreneurial mentality now will prove invaluable as you grow your business.

Part 3: Define Your Voice

"If a man does not keep pace with his companions, perhaps it is because he hears a different drummer. Let him step to the music which he hears, however measured or far away."

— Henry David Thoreau

Be Disruptive

In his acclaimed book, *The Innovator's Dilemma,* noted Harvard Business School Professor Clayton M. Christensen described his theory known as *"disruptive innovation."*[12] A disruptive innovation is one that takes an existing product that has historically been so expensive and complex that only a limited number of individuals with substantial wealth and skill have access to it and transforms it into a product that is more affordable accessible to a much larger segment of the population than previously served. [13]

The legal industry has traditionally been one that presents ease of access to the wealthy and highly educated. Aside from limited pro bono resources, the average consumer is forced to make a relatively substantial investment to afford access.

Companies like Legal Zoom, Rocket Lawyer, and Nolo have drastically increased access to legal information and quasi-legal products. Those are disruptive innovations. But, as every lawyer has at some time or another explained to his or her non-lawyer friends, those are not a substitute for an actual attorney. Do they increase accessibility to an otherwise complex product? Absolutely. But, where they fall short is in their ability to offer the reasoning and concrete advice and counsel of a traditionally trained attorney. In that regard, those companies have not disrupted the market for legal counsel, but instead for some of its by-products.

What those companies did (and did incredibly effectively) was changed the way consumers think about the definition of "legal services." But, by altering the expectations of what legal services entailed, they essentially failed to disrupt the way traditional law firms operated. Instead, they invented a new product that appealed to a previously unserved consumer segment.

So what does that mean to you as a new attorney? It means that you should continuously be striving to develop your product into one which will change the way people think about working with a lawyer and not just one that changes the way people think about the legal industry. The law is archaic and slow to change. Whether you call it a Good Ol' Boys Club or risk aversion, traditions rule the day in a profession often dictated and directed by those who live by the motto, "if it isn't broken, don't fix it."

But, the legal industry is broken. The 21st century has brought a host of changes and challenges to the profession, from an economic downturn and skyrocketing hourly rates to a more transnational and free-flowing consumer base challenged with fitting into the mold of state-specific representation, numerous factors have led to a reality no longer fitting of the system intended to serve it.

It does need to be fixed. And, the innovators that are going to fix it aren't the ones that are set in their ways and comfortable with their partner-level paychecks. The ones that are going to transform the legal industry and the way consumers work with attorneys are the entrepreneurs—the individuals with fresh new ideas for a new generation of law practice.

So as you build your business, always ask yourself what you can bring to the practice of law that will make it more accessible more convenient and more consumer-friendly. As George Bernard Shaw would say, "dream of the things that never were and ask 'why not?'"

Build a Brand

In music, every composition begins with a time signature. For the less musically inclined, the time signature is a simple notation which consists of two numbers, one over the other, which instructs the musician how to measure the beat in a piece. Quite simply, it tells the musician how to read the entire piece in front of him.

For example, take the common time signature of 3/4. Frequently seen in waltzes, the "3" indicates that there are three beats in each measure while the "4" means that the quarter note symbol is equal to one beat. The time signature is how the musician knows whether he is going to play that waltz or whether the piece is a march, a polka or the blues. It dictates how the entire piece will sound. So, while simple in its notation, a time signature carries great weight in the direction of the whole musical piece.

Your firm's brand is like a time signature. It's what makes you and your new firm distinct. It's going to tell you (and potential clients) what you are going to stand for, what the firm will look like and how you are going to conduct business.

A business without a brand is like a composition without a time signature. It's bound to come out a mess.

Think about how you want to be perceived, not only by your clients or potential clients, but by the competition, and inject that ideal into every corner of your business. From choosing colors to developing a logo; from your web design and marketing materials to the way you speak and write, your brand should be a reflection of you. It should tell your clients what they'll get when they work with you, and it will show your competition how you're different from every other lawyer.

Everything from the fonts and colors you use to create themes for your marketing and communications to the formality of your emails can psychologically affect whether your audience perceives you as relatable (and therefore, trustworthy and hireable).[14]

If you get it right, you can give yourself a leg up on the competition. Getting it wrong in the beginning means that you may find yourself challenged to dig out of a hole later on. Like a musical composition without a time signature, a business without a brand is aimless.

One of the first things I focused my time on when I opened my practice was branding. I developed everything from my firm's name, The Virtual Attorney, to the colors, slogan, and the entire brand concept for the purpose of presenting a particular image to prospective clients, my competition, and the public in general. For example, I chose orange, blue, and gray as the color scheme for my logo, website, letterhead, and other materials. Why? Well according to color theory, orange represents enthusiasm, ambitiousness, youth and vibrancy. Blue can represent steadfastness, dependability, wisdom and loyalty. Gray can be seen to represent practicality, solidarity and timelessness. Those are all virtues and traits for which I wanted others to associate with my firm. They all reflected my overall brand concept. They subtly showed consumers that The Virtual Attorney was something to be seen as accessible, convenient, modern and responsive.

And, I went further than just deciding what my colors should be. My logo, which consists of two intertwined arrows representing a "V" and an "A", is all about coming together and creating a sort of suggested space created by combining virtual technology and legal knowledge. It's meant to represent the idea that, by combining those two concepts, the client and I can create a relationship that is not constrained by traditional notions of legal representation.

When I sat down and thought about what I wanted my firm to look like, I decided that I wanted it to be a place where clients feel that they are part of the process. I wanted it to be a place where they knew they were working with a knowledgeable and friendly attorney—a n attorney with which they could be friends, but at the same time one they would confidently recommend to their parents, friends, and colleagues. I wanted clients to know and feel that they were receiving value in every aspect of the relationship and the services provided.

By articulating what I wanted my firm to be and how I wanted others to view it, I was able to create a foundation on which to build every decision affecting the company's direction. To this day, I still rely on those concepts that I defined in the infancy of my firm to guide my decision-making.

You are not going to be able to sell yourself and your services if you cannot articulate what sets you apart from the countless other firms vying for the business of your target clients. Take some time to think about it before you even bother trying to find your first client; because your brand is going to form the foundation upon which the ultimate success of your firm will be built.

Develop an Angle

What makes you exceptional? The answer to that question may not seem immediately evident, in particular for those of us that have a tenancy to see a utilitarian view of ourselves and our actions. But, that does not mean that an answer doesn't exist. Thinking about what makes you exceptional will help you stand out from the crowd.

I'll tell you a little about the angle I try to take in my own business.

I started The Virtual Attorney with the goal of bringing estate planning and business law into the 21st century. Through the use of technology, I wanted to offer a modern alternative to traditional transactional legal representation. Ultimately, my goal was to use the latest technology to provide clients with a secure, convenient, and accessible means to plan for their businesses or their estates.

But, deciding that was my objective was very different than articulating how I was going to accomplish that goal. To figure out how I was going to accomplish it, I needed to be able to lay out exactly what made me different. I needed to be able to develop and define my angle. To do so, I came up with five ways that I was going to make my firm stand out from other estate planning and business law firms.

First, I knew that I wanted to offer services at a lower cost than much of my competition. In no way did I wish to be a cheap alternative, nor did I want to compete solely on price. But, I did want lower fees to be something that set my firm apart for consumers. As a young attorney, I saw technology as a way to do that. Attorneys from my generation are so adept at using high-tech office management techniques, such as cloud file storage, online research tools, and wireless business phone systems that the need for secretaries and receptionists has dramatically decreased for many young solo attorneys and small firms. The reduction in personnel reduces overhead. Additionally, technology makes it possible to practice some types of law from virtually anywhere with cellular or Wi-Fi access. That means lower office rent costs, savings on office supplies, and more. The result is that, not only can a savvy attorney charge a lower hourly rate, but he can get the job done more efficiently and at a tremendously lower cost. That means savings for the client.

Second, it was important for consumers to view my firm as a very convenient way to get the services they needed. By structuring my firm using a virtual model, I could make myself available to clients at any time that I wasn't sleeping. In the event a client had a non-traditional schedule that required communicating with me in the evenings after kids went to bed or on Saturday mornings, I wanted to be flexible enough to make that work.

On a similar note, I wanted to be accessible. Being a younger attorney at a young law firm meant that I did not yet have an extensive portfolio of clients demanding attention. So, I wanted to be able to go above and beyond for the clients I did have by being reachable whenever there were issues and being responsive to those issues.

Fourth, I wanted to be innovative and attentive to client needs. As a young lawyer, practicing on my own, I didn't have pressure from other firm attorneys or management to do things a certain way. That meant that I could view each case uniquely without the pressure to craft a solution based on what may have worked for other clients in the past. I didn't have enough experience to get stuck in my ways, and I decided that while some people could view that as a hindrance, I saw it as an asset and something that made me stand out.

Finally, I wanted to stress the fact that a relationship with me is a lifelong relationship. I practice in areas of law where there are never resolutions. Rather, there are living solutions that continue to evolve as my clients' lives change or their businesses grow. Being a young attorney meant that I was going to be along for the ride. As grim as it sounds, it was less likely that my clients were going to outlive me as it may be if they decided to go with a more established attorney.

It's important to think about how you're different from the hordes of other attorneys out there. What may seem like hindrances to someone else can be attractive selling points to someone else. Figure out what makes you different and use it to set your firm apart from the competition.

Have Something to Say

One of the first things that many networking "pros" will tell you is that you need a honed, succinct, and formal "elevator speech." For those not familiar, an elevator speech is essentially a thirty-second marketing pitch which tells someone not only who you are, but what you do. For example, instead of saying, "Hi, I'm Mike, and I'm an attorney." An elevator speech may be something like, "Hi, I'm Mike, and I help people protect their futures and families through legal tools like wills and trusts. I also make sure that small business owners are protecting their legal interests so that they can focus on successfully growing their businesses."

Let's step back a second and think about this in the real world. I don't know about you, but frankly, when someone approaches me and starts into their elevator speech, I immediately tune out. Usually, the first thing I think about isn't how great it is that I've met you. It's, *"How the hell can I get out of this conversation?"*

Elevator speeches are not effective communication tools. They come off as stiff and rehearsed. Think about the commercials you see while watching television, specifically those local cheaply produced ones. Whether it's for a car dealership, furniture store or law office, the one thing nearly all of them have in common is obvious cue card reading. I don't know about you, but anytime I see one of those, my mind goes to the same place. I think to myself, if this place doesn't care enough about its image to even put minimal effort into its commercial, then why should I assume they put any effort or care into their product?

Every conversation you have from this point on, whether with an old friend, a crazy uncle, or even a stranger on a train is an opportunity to build a client base. That's where networking gurus have it right. But, people hate that guy that comes across like a cheap commercial, actively trying to pedal something to anyone with ears.

Can you imagine the impression you'll give if every conversation you have turns into a sales pitch? It's not pretty.

So what's the alternative?

Well, the alternative is sharing your story. Instead of lecturing people on what you do, use the opportunity to create a dialog. Talk *with* them instead of *at* them. Building a connection with someone will go much further than rattling off a rehearsed sales pitch and handing out a business card.

If you're passionate about what you do, it's going to come through in your conversations with people. When you're in business for yourself, being memorable counts. I don't want to talk to the guy who is the estate planning attorney about how he can help me avoid probate and save some money on taxes. I want to chat with him about who he is and what he likes about estate planning. I want to hear about what challenges him and why he chose to be a lawyer. Hearing his unique story is going to be far more memorable to me than listening to him try to sell me an updated will.

When you are passionate about what you do, you have something memorable to say. And when you have something memorable to say, you stay at the top of peoples' minds.

Your goal in every conversation you have from here on out isn't to sell what you do. It's to educate people and share your passion for what you do. If you can learn to do that effectively, people will remember you, and they will want to get to know you better. That's what leads to meaningful connections. So, leave the elevator pitch at home and just go out there and share your story.

Get Personal

Open up your monthly state bar journal and quickly scan the pages. Chances are pretty good that most of the legal professionals covering those pages are wearing coats and ties, sitting at big wooden desks, paging through some thick law books, or standing around with their colleagues (who are similarly dressed). I don't know why it happened, but at some point in time, the legal profession seems to have collectively decided that, to be a good lawyer and look respectable, every ounce of individualism needed to go out the window. The belief of a substantial segment of the bar, the thinking seems to go, is that clients need stereotypical lawyers that are professional and white collar.

Professionalism is a necessary characteristic of any individual practicing law, but the whole white collar image thing couldn't be farther from the truth. Of course, some clients still inevitably cling to the idea that, if their attorney doesn't wear a coat and tie or have a big office overlooking some metropolitan skyline, she must not be particularly good at her job. In reality, unless you're working with corporate clients that employ similar dress codes in their businesses, they're probably not all that impressed by coats and ties. To the contrary, that look may actually push them away.

Far worse than the stereotypical coat and tie look is the tough-mug expression so many attorneys think exudes something that clients desire. "It makes me appear to be a relentless advocate that will always fight for my clients," they'll say. Well, I think it makes you look like the last person I want to hire, and I'm sure that I'm not the only one.

I guarantee that those attorneys are throwing away thousands of dollars a year because clients, otherwise ready to hire them, don't even bother calling. Because, instead of looking like staunch advocates for their clients' interests, these attorneys end up looking cold-hearted, arrogant, and uncompassionate. Do you know what's even worse? They all look exactly the same.

If that's what you're going for (I don't know why in the world you would be), then by all means, furrow your brow, throw on a coat and tie, sit at your big wooden desk and snap the picture.

Congratulations. You just drove away potential clients while managing to look like every other attorney at the same time.

If that sounds less than ideal, then here's a better idea: *Get personal.* Be yourself. Smile. Dress how you would dress in real life.

Hiring a lawyer is about so much more than hiring someone that knows the law. A potential client is going to hire an attorney that he feels he can relate to and trust. That's likely not the tough-mugged walking coat and tie unless the potential client has an anger management problem and wants to hire someone in whom he sees himself. So, show potential clients who that person is. There is absolutely nothing wrong with meeting with a client while wearing a sweater and jeans. In all honesty, do you want to take on the client that's deciding whether to hire you based on the cost of the suit you wear to meet them? I assume the answer is no.

Getting personal goes beyond how you dress or whether you don a smile in your headshot. It goes to your brand. Think back to the chapter on building a brand. What kind of lawyer did you decide you are you going to be? You should inject that into everything you do. Whether it's writing an email without legalese or referring to your clients by their first name (and likewise encouraging your clients to refer to you by your first name), getting personal gives your clients a sense that you're just like them. It immediately makes you into someone with whom they can relate instead of what they may view as the "stereotypical attorney."

And, try using "I", "we", "us", and like terms when speaking with clients (or anyone for that matter). You need to be relatable. Don't talk about "the firm", talk about what you can do for your clients. And, try asking them about themselves, get to know them personally. The law is a profession built on trust. You can establish that quickly, and, in turn, retain great clients by relating to them instead of solely focusing on the legal issue with which they may need assistance. People hire people. Specifically, they hire people that make them feel comfortable. Make sure you show potential clients not only what you can do for them, but *who you are as a person.*

Part 4: Processing Processes

"Success is the sum of small efforts, repeated day in and day out."

— Robert Collier

Run a Business, Not a Law Firm

I get it. Lawyers run law firms. But, you're severely missing the big picture if you only think about your new company as a law firm. Your firm is a business, pure and simple. While the technical work you may do is practice law, there is much more to running a successful business than technical work.

I think this is where far too many solo attorneys fall short, and in the end, give up on their dreams of being in business for themselves. As every attorney can attest to, a legal education teaches you how to think like a lawyer, not how to be a good lawyer. And, it certainly doesn't teach you how to run a business.

To run a successful law firm—a successful business—you need to think about what you do as more than just *"practicing law."*

You need to understand your customers and what they want. You need to know how to spot weaknesses in your marketing strategy and be able to articulate the specific reasons why your services will help consumers.

Being a lawyer requires a technical know-how and an understanding of the nuances of the law. But, running a business requires an understanding of how to maximize profit by selling that expertise. It calls for an in-depth understanding of the market for your product, and how those market conditions can be used to optimize the desirability of your product over other competing products. It requires a continuous analysis of every aspect of your operations so that your business is constantly becoming more efficient, more productive, more creative, and more responsive to your customers.

Lawyers that focus on perfecting the technical aspects of practicing law will likely develop a great product, but without an emphasis on the business aspects of running a law firm that lawyer is not going to have anyone to which to sell his product. He's not going to know when his product needs to be modified or marketed differently. He's not going to know how to look at the day-to-day operations of his business and assess whether to streamline daily practices or whether standard operating procedures need to be re-evaluated. Quite simply, he is not going to know how to be successful in the business of law.

The law is an honorable profession, long held in the highest regard in western culture. But, when it comes to the business of law, it's no different than any other profession, trade, skill, or service. A baker may make the most exquisite cakes in town, but if he doesn't know how to price them appropriately or prepare them at a time of day that leaves them freshest for his customers, his brilliant baking is likely to go unnoticed. He'd be leaving potential sales on the table.

A lawyer with the most knowledge in a particular area of law or an attorney with the best oratory skills may have a far superior product over his competitors. But, if he charges too much (or too little), or if he hires support staff that lacks civility, he may not be realizing the full potential his business could realize.

Being a better technical practitioner than the competition will only get you so far when you're running your own firm. To succeed, it's imperative that you market and deliver that product to your customers effectively. It's important to know what works. And, it's essential that you realize when a change in direction might be necessary.

Try not to think of your business as a solo law firm. That mentality makes it too easy to fall into the trap of perfecting your technical skills as a lawyer without giving attention to operations, marketing, or human resources. Instead, think of yourself as a business owner. When you think of yourself as a small business owner, you turn your mind to the CEO setting. You change your mentality from one that is focused solely on product development into one focused on the big picture of operating a successful business. That is one of the most important keys to maximizing what you have to offer consumers.

Embrace technology

Going solo these days means making technology work for you. It doesn't matter whether you practice civil litigation, bankruptcy, or estate planning. There are hundreds of tools that can make your practice more efficient. That's ideal because increased efficiency leads to greater productivity and decreases costs.

Maximizing the use of efficient technologies in your business gives you the ability to automate your operations. It takes your standard operating procedures and converts them into self-sufficient processes.

Embracing technology means being proactive and continually striving to make the practice of law more manageable and more responsive to client desires. You need to understand the current cultural climate and the way your clients live. For example, your clients may expect more transparency with what's going on with their cases when, in days past, they may have been satisfied to leave things entirely in the hands of the lawyer until a final product—like a settlement offer or a completed will—was available.

Technology enables practitioners to involve clients in each step of the process no matter what it may be. Current practice management systems give attorneys the option of including access for their clients so they have full visibility into what's happening and when it's happening. Automated processes ensure that deadlines get calendared and internal firm operating procedures get followed.

Embracing technology may mean something different for you depending on the way you set up your practice. For example, I have a friend that runs his civil litigation practice out of a brick-and-mortar office. He meets with clients in the office and still files hardcopy motions and briefs with the court just as it has been done for decades. But, that doesn't mean he doesn't realize that technology can make his practice more efficient and more responsive to his clients. While between hearings, he can use his tablet to look up statutes or case law on the spot. He can use cloud-based programs to track his witness lists and notes. The availability of cloud storage enables him to condense his case file and avoid dragging heaps of papers into court with him.

His practice is a far cry from the way I operate my firm. I practice virtually, choosing to interact with clients online through video conferencing and web chat. I use cloud based storage so that I can access case information whether I'm in my office at home or a coffee shop on vacation. All of my billing and time tracking is done in the cloud as well. I use a web based phone system that permits me to receive client calls in the office or on my cell without a client having to dial multiple numbers to try to reach me. Even something as simple as syncing email over your devices increases your ability to respond to client needs promptly. In turn, that enhances the customer experience. My goal is to make every task one that can be done from anywhere, and even if that's not yours, it's important for you to think about how you can use technology to your advantage.

While very different in form, both my practice and my friend's practice use technology to improve the client experience. My friend's clients appreciate his ability to access any part of the case file quickly with a few swipes of the finger. My clients appreciate the convenience and accessibility of being able to work with me remotely without having to take time out of their busy lives to make room for working with an attorney.

Whether it's using cloud-based accounting and reporting software or using a virtual secretarial service available 24 hours a day, technology is going to make your business run smoother from an operations standpoint. Not only is that going to increase the clients' overall experiences while working with you, but it's going to free up your time so you can focus on their cases.

A law firm doesn't need much more than the lawyer himself to operate. However, to be successful, it's necessary to incorporate tools that increase productively and improve the level of service. Never before in history has there been a time where technology has been so cheap (many times even free) and so prevalent. Embrace that reality.

When you make a commitment to maximize the use of efficient technologies in your business you make a commitment to yourself that you'll continually strive to do better, and you make a commitment to your clients that your firm will do whatever it takes to improve their experience and maximize the outcome it delivers.

Streamline Everything

Embracing technology is an essential concept for any new law firm in this day in age. As a solo attorney, you can make your job considerably easier by using that technology to streamline and automate time-consuming processes. By doing so, you'll be able to free yourself from the time and energy drain caused by the many mundane, but necessary tasks associated with the operation of any successful business.

An initial focus on streamlining business operations may seem unnecessary for the solo attorney with few clients and ample time to dedicate to business operations and administrative work. But, it's important to realize that, while growth doesn't happen overnight, it does have a tenancy to sneak up on you. I promise that if you stay in the game, your firm will grow. Preemptively streamlining your business will enable you to approach that growth proactively and use it as a springboard for further advancement.

Beginning with day one, you need to make a habit of assessing your firm's operational efficiency. Make a habit of regularly asking yourself three questions:

First, "On what actions am I spending my time?"

Second, "What am I getting in return for the time and effort invested in those actions?"

And third, "What can I do to decrease that time and effort and increase the outcomes?"

Those questions will help you pinpoint the areas where there is a disconnect between the time and energy you are putting into a particular task and the return you see from that effort regardless of how it's measured.

Take an example. Let's say that you've spent considerable time developing a comprehensive marketing strategy for your firm. As part of that plan, you've decided that social media engagement will be one of your primary marketing channels because it's a relatively inexpensive way to reach a particular target demographic. But, as everyone is keenly aware, social media is a rapidly developing communication medium. With the popularity of various platforms changing frequently and new variants popping up regularly, there's a lot to keep track of. What may be popular today may be an afterthought tomorrow (for example, look at the rapid decline of MySpace's popularity in the 2000's).

There are so many trends and changes to keep track of that maintaining an effective social media marketing strategy has become an actual career in many larger companies. Maintaining an engaging presence on every social media channel would be practically impossible for a solo attorney that has to wear dozens of other hats without some useful streamlining tools.

Using a social media management system is a way to automate that social media marketing strategy. There are handfuls of cloud-based software programs designed for that exact purpose. So, instead of constantly maintaining a presence on every single popular social media platform, a solo attorney can consolidate those efforts into a centralized program which will actively engage with various social media platforms without the need for continual oversight.

All of a sudden, a cornerstone of the marketing efforts which used to take ten hours a week now may take only a couple. That means that there's more time to focus on other things, like actually being a lawyer.

Constantly aim to streamline every aspect of your business. Continually look for ways to do things simpler, smarter, cheaper and faster without sacrificing quality and you'll ensure that you maximize your bottom line. If those streamlined processes are reliable they are going to facilitate your firm's growth.

Master Basic Accounting Skills

The chances are good that you have at least some knowledge of basic accounting principles already, even if that knowledge is incredibly limited. When you start a business, you don't need to become an expert in accounting principles. However, you do need to know enough to assess whether the business is growing, how fast it's doing so, and whether that is a sufficient speed to ensure that you're able to stay afloat while you develop a client base and predictable stream of revenue.

Learning the basics of accounting probably sounds like a no-brainer in the list of essential skills to know if you want to run a successful business. After all, the primary objective of any business is to make a profit. If you don't know how to read the numbers and analyze them to determine whether that's happening your company is not going to say afloat. But, it's far too easy to overthink every detail of your finances if you don't have the appropriate tools with which to measure those details.

Without knowledge of things like profit and loss statements, cash flow, and various types of expenses, it's impossible to assess the financial health of your business with any degree of accuracy. The only alternative is to look at how much money is in your bank account. While that bottom line is important, a fixation with it can be discouraging. There are too many variables that go into operating a successful company—even a small one—that can't be accounted for without other tools.

So, it's important to have the skills necessary to assess growth in various ways. For example, how did the business do in one quarter compared to another? Did you sell more of a particular type of service? Maybe your profit was down, but did you help a higher volume of clients? Did you do paid work for more returning clients?

You should be able to look at a balance sheet and profit and loss statement and realize how you're spending your money and where your big expenses are coming from. But, try not to get too caught up with every little expense. You should look at your books and records with an eye towards gauging where progress is being made and where the most promising places for improved growth may be. Obsessing over finances will drain you mentally. Dwelling on every penny is going to suck the energy out of you and your delicate new operation, because the fact of the matter is, unless you're an extreme outlier, the outlook is going to be bleak in the beginning.

Use accounting skills to find various ways to measure your progress as a business owner aside from the bottom line to give yourself positive encouragement. Even if monthly profits aren't what you thought they should be, or an examination of your financial statements doesn't support your initial projections, knowing how to analyze the financials will give you insights into why the business is the way it is. That's essential to assessing your company's current situation and determining where to focus your energy going forward.

Instead of panicking about what the books say, glance at the big picture and move on. You're better off using your energy to go out and grow your practice.

Define Your "Measurables"

Monetary metrics, like those gleaned through a careful analysis of your financials, are obviously helpful when gauging the health of your business. But, as I've already explained, relying solely on the bottom line can be risky. Relying purely on financial metrics misses the bigger picture. Sure, the numbers will show you whether you're bringing in a profit and where your expenses are coming from, but without more, you aren't going to be able to create a clear picture of how and why your numbers say what they say.

You need to define and design your measurables in a way that gives you that *"how"* and *"why."*

Think about which metrics are going to show you the health of your business. Financial metrics are a start if you know how to use them. But what else? You need to figure out how to organize data in a way that you can understand it, realize what it says about the health of your practice, analyze it, and use it to fuel growth.

Any MBA student can give you a canned response on what you need to be measuring and how you need to be doing it. To many traditionally educated business students, there are right and wrong ways to measure a business's success. But to stay motivated and organized, I'd encourage you to set standards that work for you, and measure those standards in ways that are easy for you to understand and learn from. They don't need to be conventional. Remember this is your company. Don't worry about what the rest of the business world does or even what other solos do. Do what works for you.

Remember that every standard operating procedure or metric used by businesses to measure growth came from somewhere. Just because it's commonplace now doesn't mean it was widely accepted when it was first implemented someplace.

Back in 1985, Motorola began adopting an approach pioneered by Toyota with the goal of improving the measure of quality of their products and operations called Six Sigma. At a very high level, Six Sigma centers on using data-driven processes and methodologies to eliminate defects with the aim of improving the overall operations of a company. Motorola developed the process to better understand where it was falling short and how to alleviate shortfalls present in its products and processes. It was not until the 1990s, when Jack Welch, the famed CEO of General Electric made it central to GE's internal organizational operation that it became a more generally accepted method for improving business efficiencies.[15]

The point is that Motorola decided it needed to develop processes which provided more clarity about where the company's operations were falling short. Instead of following traditional models of metric measurement up to that point, the company developed something that was uniquely tailored to pinpoint its own issues. Six Sigma is now a well-accepted (though admittedly sometimes criticized) method of measuring efficiency and improving operations at some of the world's largest corporations.

As was done by the folks at Motorola, you need to figure out what works for you.

It doesn't have to be the adoption of complex systems or invention of new metrics. It can be as simple as organizing data in a way that helps you understand where you can focus the very limited time and resources you have with the objective of maximizing the return on that invested energy.

For example, when I started my firm I realized that I needed a quick and easy way to understand where the few valuable clients I had were coming from (because, naturally, I wanted more of them). So what did I do? I plugged some information like client names, locations, and the services I provided to each into simple spreadsheets. I'm a visual learner, so I color coded the entire thing, using different colors for different areas of law, geographic locations and acquisition source. This simple method allowed me to see where business was coming from and where I should focus my energy. I quickly realized that most of my clients were coming from a very specific type of referral source. So, I invested my time and energy in learning how I could increase my involvement with that group of sources to develop more meaningful relationships, and in turn, more paying clients.

I developed metrics based on that data and used those metrics to set goals for improvements that I wanted to see. I used those spreadsheets for years while my practice gained a footing to track my money and my time.

Whether you base your metrics off of a readily accepted business practice used by some of the world's largest corporations, or use color-coded spreadsheets, find ways that enable you to measure how and why your business is going the direction it is going. And, make sure to do it in a way that works for you. The numbers are important, but without actually looking at the "how" and "why" behind the numbers, you won't know what needs to be done to change them.

Part 5: Make it a Lifestyle

"Dream and give yourself permission to envision a you that you choose to be."

— Joy Page

Screw Social Norms

Running your own business comes with a multitude of mental challenges that are absent in a traditional career. One of the most challenging parts of starting your own business is grasping that realization. Running a new business isn't a traditional career choice. It's not a "nine-to-fiver." It's a lifestyle.

While your friends may be able to go home at 5:00 pm and tune out thoughts of work until the next morning, you're going to need to be available continuously to tend to whatever issues may arise. That may be disheartening, but that doesn't mean that you need to work constantly. It just means you need to be ready to work whenever the situation calls for it. I can guarantee that you'll be working full-time, even if that doesn't mean you'll be working the same hours every day.

There may be days when there's nothing that absolutely *has* to be done. There will be days that you'll find yourself scanning Netflix at 1:00 pm while scrolling through Twitter in your pajamas. And, it's going to feel strange. You're going to feel like you're doing something wrong. If you had a traditional job, you certainly would be doing something wrong. But, being your own boss isn't a traditional job. Assuming that you have had one of those at some point in your life, I know that you'll probably feel a little guilty binge watching Breaking Bad in the middle of a Wednesday afternoon instead of grinding away at your desk. That holds especially true if you have a spouse with a traditional career. But, that's the tradeoff for making yourself available to jump into action at a moment's notice anytime a business issue or client concern needs attention. You may find yourself tending to an emergency a few nights later which keeps you working until 11:00 pm. It will all even out, so you might as well embrace the freedom inherent in this lifestyle.

I had an economics professor in college who told the class on the first day, "If you wake up and sincerely believe that your time is better spent doing something else, I don't want you to waste it coming to my class." That's wonderful advice for life but a risky proposition for a group of young college students. Suffice it to say; I took that professor up on his offer more times than not and unsurprisingly didn't do that well in his class. But, the point stuck with me, and I regularly think back on it as I build my business.

There are days I wake up and decide that sitting at my desk lazily fumbling through administrative work isn't going to be the best use of my time. So instead, I'll go for a long walk to get the creative juices flowing and clear my mind. Just because I'm not sitting in front of a computer doesn't mean that my activities aren't directly related to the growth of my business. As my own boss, I get to decide that those activities are essential for me to stay at my best and avoid falling into a rut. If you decide that the best use of your time is spending the day recharging the old batteries, then by all means, you should do it.

You can decide that you're going to feel guilty about taking an unplanned afternoon off or stretching your lunch break out by a few hours. Or, you can choose to do what I finally learned to do when those non-traditional work days inevitably arose.

You can say, "*Screw it.*"

Remember, that you are starting your own business because you want something different. If you wanted the traditional lifestyle that family, friends, and society stereotypically view as normal, you would have gone after it. But, the reality is that you're starting your own business. You get to make the rules. You get to decide how your professional life is going to balance with your personal life.

Believe me, it's an incredibly daunting challenge to forget about what other people may think about your day-to-day professional life. Frankly, I think it's the single biggest challenge you'll face. But, you're wasting your time if you don't. The people that personally matter to you are going to see that you're happy doing what you're doing. They're going to see that you're serious about making a life for yourself that is fulfilling and fruitful. They are going to respect that you have chosen to follow your heart and build something that lets you live the way you want to live.

If you felt that you needed to be like everyone else, you would be working in a traditional job like everyone else. But, you don't want to be like everyone else. You crave to be something more, something different, and something unique. Don't forget that, even when others may think your desire is misguided.

Forget what others may think. The only person whose opinion matters in this whole thing is yours. If you sincerely believe that what you're doing to build your business is the best thing you can be doing to build your business, do it. You're the boss for a reason.

Redefine "The Job"

The expectation that every adult should work (at minimum) a 40-hour per week job has become ingrained in American culture. As a people, we look upon working long hours like a badge of honor. We tend to assume that, if we have free time, we must not be as successful as our colleagues. Taking a Tuesday afternoon off work to go to a baseball game or enjoying March Madness in front of your television without your laptop fired up is frowned upon by many.

While working long hours is certainly not unique to Americans, it is done more frequently in the United States when compared to the average democratic market-based economy.[16] As a culture, Americans tend to view working long hours as something of a necessity, an obligation of which fulfillment is necessary to be viewed by society as "*normal*."[17]

The problem I have with the traditional American view of work is that it's something which lives are built around and not something built around lives. If you're a male, the issue is likely exacerbated by deeply rooted ideas of masculine responsibility and stereotypical assumptions about gender. And, if you're a female, there may be a sense that you need to work extra hard to make up for the unfortunate inequality present in the American workplace due to decades of gender discrimination. For many, the amount of work one performs represents a badge of honor and, whether fair or not, a measure of an individual's passion, commitment, and drive.

There are plenty of professionals that go against the grain and instead approach work with a very different idea of how it should fit into a person's life. For those mold-breakers, working long hours and sacrificing personal opportunities for professional gain isn't an option. They have decided that, while work is a necessary and substantial part of life, what defines them as people is how they take that necessity and mold it into something that creates the lives they want to live instead of letting it mold them into what cultural expectations may dictate those lives should look like.

Unless you have previously started your own business, you're going to quickly find that working for yourself is nothing like any job you have ever had before. It will become immediately apparent that what you call "*work*" is vastly different than what your peers and fellow (non-solo) legal colleagues call it.

Even though the balance of your professional and personal life may not be at the mercy of a well-established enterprise, starting and building your own firm is going to consume you. Whether it's driving ninety minutes to meet a new client on Saturday evening or simply sitting at a coffee shop for hours on end brainstorming new marketing and client acquisition strategies, you'll have no shortage of work. But, that work is not going to be what your peers think of as work.

Your job is not going to involve sitting in a cubicle from 8:00AM-5:00PM with a thirty-minute afternoon escape to the cafeteria. Sure, you're going to spend days at the courthouse shuffling from appearance to appearance or consulting prospective clients all morning and then logging six hours in the afternoon drafting employment agreements. But, you're also going to have days where you don't do any client work until 2:00PM because you spent the morning working on your marketing plan or playing golf with a prospective client.

Working that way requires you to change your definition of the job. It requires you to scrap all of those social axioms that define work in American culture and deeply ingrained assumptions about what work should and should not be. It forces you to ignore your condemnatory cubicle-dwelling friends, who in reality are probably envious of the flexibility your lifestyle affords you.

The simple truth is that you'll probably work more than them and harder than them because you have no other choice. That's because unlike most of them, when your work is substandard you aren't going to get a "talking to" by your boss. In solo practice, when your work isn't up to snuff your business is going to fail. It's as simple as that. Golf with that client may sound fun, but when your next paycheck depends on convincing your golf partner to hire you to revamp his company's executive compensation structure, you may find yourself wishing you were sitting in an office somewhere writing memos or filing SEC forms like your friends.

While you may not work the same way as your peer—or even define "work" the same way—it's important that you realize those folks are probably just not going to understand what building a business— specifically, building a law firm—involves. Regardless, remember this: what you do with your workday isn't wrong just because it's not traditional. That mindset is essential to maintaining a positive outlook on what you've chosen to do with your career.

Redefine what the word "*job*" means to you. Don't feel guilty that you aren't staring at your computer screen for nine hours every weekday. You're starting your own business so that you can balance life on your terms and not those of society.

Show Up to Work

Just because you have the freedom to decide your daily schedule doesn't mean that you're necessarily going to have any more free time or any less work than your friends with traditional jobs. As I've said, you should use that freedom and flexibility to decide the best way to spend each day with the goal of finding the most effective ways to build your business. But, that doesn't mean that you should wake up each day without a plan. Your time is finite, and figuring out how to use it efficiently will lead to success.

Unlike your peers that work for someone else, you not only need to perform the technical "*lawyering*" work of being an attorney with excellence, but you are required to make sure the business is operationally sound as well. That means that you'll need to deal with vendors of practice management and data storage solutions. You'll need to research and schedule networking events, lunches, coffees, meet-and-greets, and the like. You're going to have to keep track of trust account, advertising, compliance with ethics rules, business registrations, licensing, tax preparation and estimated payments, scheduling consultations, content marketing (if you decide to engage in it), social media policies and engagement, and dozens of other tasks that may be managed by administrative staff or delegated to specific attorneys at other firms.

The point is there will be plenty of various tasks that you'll need to do every day, all of which require very different skills and approaches.

While you have the flexibility to prioritize things, planning to make time for all of them is essential to operating an efficient practice. While you may get to decide when they get done, things will be a whole lot easier if you build some structure into your work day. You may not have a boss looking over your shoulder making sure that you show up on time in the morning, but if you approach each day like one is, you'll set yourself up for success.

I have three simple rules that I set for myself when it came to structuring my approach to work days:

1) Always set hours.

2) Get dressed.

3) Show up.

Set hours for yourself.

It doesn't matter what they are but they should be consistent. Make them 8:00AM-5:00PM with a lunch break at noon if you have a spouse that works traditional hours so you can relax with him or her in the evenings. If you have children who you need to get up and out the door to school in the morning, don't start your day until later. Or, if you have clients that find it easiest to meet or chat in the evenings after they get off work, then build your schedule around that.

My wife doesn't work on Tuesdays. To spend time with her, I typically try to work 7:30AM-5:30PM, Monday, Wednesday, Thursday, and Friday. It works for me, but you may find you're not that terrible productive working only four days per week. That's fine. Set the schedule that works for your life. Just make it a point to follow it, whatever it may be.

No one's perfect. There may be days when your schedule doesn't work out, but by making a conscious effort to keep the same regular hours you'll establish a habit of maximizing productivity.

More importantly, setting hours will enable you to separate yourself from your work instead of letting it consume you. Sure, there are going to be nights when you'll need to work or Sundays when things just need to get done, but making a habit out of setting down the smart phone every evening creates a boundary. Without it, you run the risk of losing the freedom gained by starting your own firm in the first place.

Get Dressed.

That sounds so simple it could go without saying, right? Some people have this weird assumption that other people only like putting on clothes because they absolutely have to. I've never understood it. The last thing I want to do on a weekend, yet alone on a Monday morning when I have fifteen different things to get done, is sit around unshowered in sweatpants and a t-shirt. I don't know if I'm in the minority or what, but people seem really confused when I laugh off the seemingly accepted assumption that life is so much better in pajamas. Frankly, the thought of sitting around in lounge clothes on a work day has never even crossed my mind.

I can't say it enough. Working for yourself still means *working*, and if you want to be successful at being your own boss, you need to take it seriously. You don't need to sit around your office in a coat and tie, but pull yourself together in the morning.

There is a continually evolving body of research which suggests that the clothes we wear have a direct psychological effect on our self-perception. Termed "*enclothed cognition*" by researchers at Northwestern University, the phenomenon is changing the way we need to think about our outward appearance.[18]

The researchers, Hajo Adam and Adam Galinsky, performed a series of experiments to test their hypothesis that, not only do the clothes individuals wear have an effect on how others see them, but they have an actual effect on the way those individuals perceive themselves.

In one of the most telling experiments, subjects were randomly assigned either a white lab coat or street clothes. Wearing their selected articles, they were then asked to perform a series of simple identification tasks on a computer screen by identifying the name of a color. Color names were displayed randomly in red ink or blue ink, some congruous ("RED" appearing in red ink or "BLUE" appearing in blue ink), and some incongruous ("RED" appearing in blue ink or vice versa). Subjects were asked to identify the color being spelled out. The results showed that the subjects wearing street clothes made nearly twice as many errors in identifying the incongruous results as those subjects wearing the lab coats.[19]

So, while it has been known for some time that "dressing for the job you want" may increase your chances of being hired or promoted, the clothes you wear may also have a direct correlation with the quality of the work you perform.

Show up.

Setting hours for yourself is pointless unless you actually show up ready to work. Like any other job, set goals for your day. Make sure that you organize your daily activities around the priorities you've set for the firm. It's important to give yourself measurable benchmarks against which to mark your performance and efficiency for a day, week, or month, because unlike your peers, you don't have a supervisor determining what those objectives need to be. Again, blowing a day off here or there is fine. It's fine because you decide it's fine. Physically showing up every day isn't a necessity, but when you do, mentally showing up is essential. When you're at work, you should be fully committed to productivity.

Working for yourself can be tremendously liberating, but if you're not careful that freedom can be detrimental to both you and your business. While you may not have a traditional job, try treating yours like one. It'll pay off in the long run.

Always Start Something

I assume that, at some point in your life, you've had a job working for someone else—a job where you were told what to do and when to do it. At least for me, sometimes the best days at those jobs were the ones where there were very few things that had to be done.

"Great," you'd think. "I get to sit around and catch up on all the pictures of babies my friends have posted to Facebook."

There's no doubt that those unanticipated days can make for pleasant surprises since they break up the daily grind of a nine-to-five job. But, where you are your own boss, you tend to view them a bit differently. Those days still come around from time to time when you work for yourself. The big difference, of course, is that no one is paying you to sit around.

When I started my firm, I quickly found that, after sitting down at my desk, answer a few emails, checking the status of my cases, and getting some administrative tasks out of the way for the day, sometimes I wouldn't have anything that I *had* to do. Whether it was because I was in a holding pattern waiting for a client to review documents I previously sent over, or just one of those breaks where I was waiting for new work to come in, there were (and still are) times every now and then when I could just as easily have closed my inbox for the day, shut off my phone, and literally gone for a hike.

Tempting? Sure. But, if I decided to do that then I would be giving up a valuable opportunity to grow the business, and growing your business should be your constant objective.

I keep three lists of to-do items for when I get those lulls in the real business of being a lawyer:

1) Firm Improvement
2) Lawyer Improvement
3) Self-Improvement

Each list is a compilation of tasks that I can turn to when I have breaks in the lawyering part of the job so that I'm continually improving my business, my skills, my knowledge as a practitioner, and my personal well-being.

For example, the "*Firm Improvement*" list may include items like: "develop a marketing strategy directed at a new niche," "set up lunches or morning coffee with interesting community members or other professionals to increase my network," and, "develop more streamlined processes for client engagement, response time and interaction."

The "*Lawyer Improvement*" category may include things like: "study the new Wisconsin Trust Code" and "attend a continuing legal education seminar."

The "*Self-Improvement*" list may consist of tasks like: "explore potential business opportunities ancillary to the firm," "set new health and fitness goals for the next year," and "go for a long run to clear my head and recharge."

When business is slow I look to my list and I make it a goal always to start something. Because, when you decide you're going to take a proactive approach to tackling downtime, you're making a commitment to continual self-improvement. Wasting a day when there isn't anything to do is certainly a nice break, but it doesn't move your business forward. So always try to start something.

It may seem tacky, but I always try to tell myself, "Blowing off today is sure to lead you to tomorrow, but using today to improve yourself or your business may lead you to somewhere you can't even imagine."

Whether that's developing as an attorney, growing my business, or simply improving my personal well-being, the moments when the obligations of work aren't getting in the way of life create opportunities that you should try to maximize.

So, always ask yourself, "What can I be doing right now to become better?" That will ensure that you're maximizing the opportunities with which you are presented to move the business forward.

Always Learn

One incredibly beneficial thing you can do with some of that downtime is learn. Maximize the advantage that you're getting out of everything you do by continually striving to acquire knowledge. Whether that's by learning a new accounting technique that will help you more efficiently track your income, learning a new area of law or expanding your knowledge base on an existing practice area, or researching ways to improve client experience, you will accelerate your firm's growth by constantly learning.

When I was in law school, I had an adjunct professor that taught a class on S Corporation and Partnership Taxation—certainly not an easy subject (not to mention one that even most lawyers find incredibly boring and mundane). The class met from 6:00PM-9:00PM on Tuesday nights, which made it all that much more dreadful, at least to the students.

The professor loved it.

It should come as no surprise that I, like probably every other student in the class, was just baffled that anyone in their right mind would enjoy such a subject, and enjoy it so much so that he wanted to spend his Tuesday evenings teaching it to a bunch of law students. There were times while I was sitting in that class when the thought of spending the night organizing my sock drawer seemed like an attractive alternative. Seemingly aware of that reality, one evening he shared with the class the reason he enjoyed immersing himself in complicated tax law and sharing his knowledge with others. He said the reason was, quite simply that he learned something new every day.

Subchapter K of the United States Tax Code contains only about thirty sections. It is surprisingly simple in its drafting (at least for someone with a little experience reading tax law), yet its application can pose some of the most complex tax conundrums to businesses. My professor enjoyed the challenges that came along with that complexity. He had been a practicing tax attorney for over twenty years at that point and still insisted that he left work every day with some tidbit of knowledge about the application and interpretation of the body of law surrounding Subchapter K that he didn't have when he showed up that morning.

The explanation he gave about his passion for partnership taxation has stuck with me to this day because it offers an illustration of the power of constantly seeking knowledge. At his core, my professor's enthusiasm for learning was what drove him to continually grow as an attorney.

It's obvious you aren't going to know everything there is to know about your area of law or running a business. You know that. But, what you should remember is that it's OK not to know everything as long as you capitalize on the opportunities you have to build on the knowledge you do have.

Continual learning leads to a number of personal and professional benefits. There have been numerous studies done that show, amongst other things, that continued education in adulthood increases verbal ability, memory, and fluency,[20] can increase motivation, improve attitude and empower individuals,[21] result in improved job performance,[22] increase innovation, improve self-management skills, and increase planning effectiveness.[23]

Make it a goal to continually learn new skills and expand your knowledge of the things that interest you. Doing so will not only improve your business, but it will lead to personal growth as well.

Part 6: Selling Yourself

"Don't let what you cannot do interfere with what you can do."

— John R. Wooden

Get Out There

My firm is The Virtual Attorney, and as the name suggests, it's a virtual law firm. For those not familiar with virtual law firms, they essentially maximize the use of technology to create convenience and accessibility for clients by reducing the need for in-person engagement.

I'll be the first to admit that, when I started the firm, I overestimated the effect my online presence was going to have on my client acquisition success. I naively thought that, since the firm was virtual, potential clients would find me on Google or Bing or Facebook, or whatever platform, and flock to me in droves. My business was going to be an instant success off the bat, I thought, all thanks to the power of the internet!

As you can probably guess, that's not exactly how things played out. I did have a fair amount of success getting people to my firm's website to learn about me and my services. But, getting people to sign up to pay me—someone they have never met and know very little about—a substantial amount of money was a different story. After all, sharing incredibly specific and highly sensitive details about one's family, financial situation, morals, values and personal life is unsurprisingly not something that many people do lightly. Who knew?

A change in marketing tactics was inevitable if I wanted any chance of succeeding in the business of law.

I had to get out there and network.

There are plenty of resources available that can teach you about networking, and I won't pretend this is one of those. But, whether you have a Type A personality and welcome the opportunity to talk to anybody, or you're an introvert to whom the thought of walking into a crowded room of strangers and engaging in conversation seems worse than death, your success as a solo attorney will directly relate to how many people you know. Whether you call it networking, rubbing elbows, or making new friends, you need to get out there and expand your database of connections.

Networking in the traditional sense, that is, attending events where strangers put on name tags and force small talk with each other is not my favorite pastime. Of course, that doesn't mean I don't put on a smile and do it. But, I knew from the start that wasn't my ideal way to meet people. So instead, I would go straight to setting up one-on-one meetings with people. Doing so comes with advantages over traditional group networking. It gives me an opportunity to have an actual conversation, learn a little about the other person, share my story, and have a chance for a genuine connection upon which I could build over time.

When I first started inviting people to have lunch or sit down for coffee before heading off to the office, I stayed within my comfort zone. I had little interest in meeting completely new people, but rather made it a goal to grow the relationships I already had but may not have invested in as much as I would have liked. But, slowly I branched out and expanded my reach to include complete strangers.

What I learned was that I enjoyed sitting down with someone I didn't know that well or hadn't spoken to in ten years. I enjoyed learning about where they'd been and how they'd gotten there. That realization led me to expand my horizons from a networking perspective.

Now, I have no problem sending a quick message to the author of an interesting article that I read in the local paper, or reaching out to other established attorneys in my practice areas to build relationships. And, that's all networking is—building relationships. The key for me was finding what I liked doing instead of doing what everyone else said I should be doing.

When you stop approaching networking with the goal of drumming up business and drop the "what can this person do for me" mentality, you'll realize that, by learning about other people, you're developing a web of connections that is going to prove invaluable to your business. Whether that means doing the one-on-one thing or the traditional networking event thing, do what works for you.

Remember that you're not out fishing for referral sources. You're out developing a network and building relationships.

So, my one piece of networking advice is just to get out there. Figure out what works for you and what you enjoy. Learn for yourself how you enjoy connecting with people and do it.

You May Be a Small Fish, but It's a Small Pond

Entering the legal profession as a rough-edged newbie can be incredibly intimidating for plenty of reasons, not the least of which is the challenge of establishing your new firm's place in the market when so many seasoned and established practitioners already have strong footholds in the industry.

Knowing where to start and developing an effective plan for client acquisition can seem overwhelming. If the thought of getting your firm to the point where it has a consistent flow of new clients and matters sufficient to financially support you seems overwhelming and intimidating, it doesn't have to be. At least from my experience, it only seems daunting because of the lens through which you're viewing the situation.

I know that at some point you've said the following to yourself:

> "How in the world am I going to find clients when I have no name recognition, no practical legal experience, and when other lawyers have been doing it for thirty years?"

Those concerns are completely understandable for any new attorney. Frankly, it's natural for any freshly-minted graduate in any profession to have similar worries. Like anything, keeping a reasonable perspective about the future and developing realistic expectations is practically impossible without any frame of reference against which to measure your assumptions. But, here's what you have to remember: Every attorney that came before you had to start somewhere too. Establishing a name for yourself in an established industry is never easy, but it's easier today than it ever has been.

The internet and social media have drastically shrunk the world. No longer is your sphere of influence limited to your city or region. Now, instead of reaching potential clients through publications, phonebooks, and billboards, you can reach an audience of thousands by blasting out 140 characters from your smartphone.

What you need to do is characterize your target market. Remember earlier when you thought about who your ideal client was? You need to focus on targeting that demographic as well as the other professionals that serve that group, no matter how small. Personally, I think the more you can tailor your definition of your ideal client, the more effective you will be.

Here's why.

Targeting a narrowly-focused core demographic is going to make you memorable within that group and responsive to what it wants. That's going to make your product desirable. When you have an alluring product—one which is responsive to what clients are looking for—it becomes an industry standard for that crowd. All of a sudden, you've established your place in the market by focusing on what a very particular group wants in a lawyer. I'm oversimplifying this, of course. But, the takeaway is that, when you can reclassify your ultimate goals into more focused objectives, the road becomes much more manageable.

Now, I'm certainly not saying that sending out a few tweets is going to make you a successful solo or even lead directly to a single potential client. What I am saying is that you have channels at your disposal that enable you to gain a footing and establish yourself as a familiar voice in your niche practice area. Demonstrating your knowledge and passion for the law will (slowly) lead to established credibility amongst the very community you may have initially been so challenged to break into.

Think for a minute about Facebook. Now open to everyone (and quite literally their mothers), Facebook didn't start as a social media platform for the masses. Instead, it was started simply as an online profile directory of students at a single university. Initially only open to Harvard students, Facebook aimed to create a sense of community amongst the Ivy League school's pupils—a *"who's who"* directory of headshots, relationship statuses, and other personal details. Through little more than word-of-mouth, after the first month of its existence, over half of Harvard's students were signed up on Facebook. It eventually spread to Colombia, Stanford and Yale before opening up to the rest of the Ivy League schools, and the rest is history.[24]

Facebook started small and selective. That led to a sense of prestige amongst the Harvard students who were initially the only ones allowed to sign up. Mark Zuckerberg went fishing in a small pond when he started Facebook at Harvard.

What Facebook can teach a new business owner is that by focusing their product in on a select group of people and creating a sense of inclusiveness, Facebook was able to establish itself as something that students felt they needed to use in order to belong. The site became the social media platform of choice for college students swiftly developing an identity for itself as Myspace for the college-educated crowd.

Facebook didn't grow into a necessary part of identity for college students (and subsequently everyone else) with multi-million dollar advertising campaigns or angel investors (at least at the beginning). It did so by creating a product that every one of a certain age and certain educational background felt they needed. Once the base was built, the business organically expanded because of what it stood for.[25]

When you go fishing in a small pond, it's easier to figure out where to drop your line to make the fish bite. Just like Mark Zuckerberg at Harvard, as a newly minted solo attorney, you need to view yourself as the fisherman at that small pond.

As a solo lawyer, the reality is that you don't need a potential market base of thousands of people. Depending on your area of legal expertise you may be able to find success with only a handful of clients. Define what it is you're selling and who it is you're selling to. Establishing yourself as a prominent voice for even a small group will lead to success.

Be Picky

When you're just starting out as a new solo attorney, it's exciting anytime the phone rings, because it means a potential new client may be in your future. But, many times a consult with that new potential client reveals a case that may be flawed. By that, I don't mean a case that may pose a challenge factually. You can handle those (in practice, those are the cases that really allow you to use your skill as a practitioner). When I say flawed, I'm talking about something else. There are some clients that, though they may want to hire you, are more trouble than they're worth. In the long run taking on those clients can be detrimental to the growth of your firm.

Whether it's a client that has trouble sharing the whole truth with you, a client that tries to negotiate on fees, a client that has a hard time communicating with you in a timely manner, or a client with a case outside your area of expertise, flawed clients come with much more risk than potential reward.

It's tempting to be a *"Yes Man (or Woman)"* and accept every new potential client that comes calling, but that can have potentially disastrous consequences in more ways than one.

First, it can be a drain on your resources. Every time you need to immerse yourself in the intricacies of a new area of law simply to represent one client, it takes away from the time you can be spending with other clients, in marketing your firm towards quality potential clients, in developing your product, and in growing your business.

Second, it waters down your product. When you take any case that walks through the door, you're weakening your position as an expert in a particular field and confusing potential referral sources on exactly what you do.

When you talk with a new potential referral source and tell him that you practice estate planning for families with children, but you're happy to take on DUI or family law cases as well, what does that say about your product? If another attorney said that to me, I'd think she was desperate for clients and quality representation may be taking a backseat to simply getting paid by anyone. It would tell me that attorney was not an expert on anything. In such a case, not only is that potential referral source going to question whether you're the best fit for DUI and family law cases, but he is probably going to question whether you're even an ideal referral source for estate planning cases. He's going to walk away from that conversation wondering what is that you really do.

Third, taking on flawed clients potentially opens you up to negative client reviews, and more seriously, possible malpractice claims. As they say, reputation is everything. Imperfect clients have already developed expectations for the outcomes of their cases even before you agree to take them on. Most of the time those expectations are unreasonable given the facts presented. It's a losing proposition for you. You simply won't be able to live up to their expectations or provide satisfactory outcomes for them.

Think about it. Who is more likely to leave a review of your services? Is it the client that had an excellent experience with you or the one that was left entirely unsatisfied? One negative review is going to make your job of building a reputation as a competent expert that much harder. It's up to you whether you'll take those clients on, but to me, it's not worth the risk.

Finally, working with flawed clients is mentally draining. It's impossible to satisfy a bad client with a bad case because her expectations are unrealistic from the beginning.

One of the benefits of having your own business is getting to decide who you are going to work for. So, save yourself the trouble and learn how to say no. Develop criteria and best practices for the type of client you are going to work with and turn away the clients that don't fit within those parameters.

By sticking to your guns and learning to say no to clients that don't fit your ideal mold, you will free yourself to do great work for the clients that do. By doing so, you are going to strengthen your brand, your business, and your reputation.

Target Passionate People

Growing a successful and sustainable business requires building a customer base that is substantial enough to produce new referrals consistently, and that base needs to be engaged frequently enough to generate consistent sales. That's certainly not a concept unique to law firms by any stretch of the imagination. But, due to some unique constraints around ethics and marketing that we all know too well, it does pose more of a challenge than it would if you were just opening up an online clothing shop or a landscaping business.

So up front, it's important to spend some time developing a plan for how you may build that customer base. The thought of developing a model that is sustainable and profitable in the long term can be intimidating, to say the least. But, just like every other aspect of your firm, breaking it down systematically and articulating some core principals from which to drive your growth is essential.

When it came to developing my growth plan, I found it helpful to do three things:

1) I thoroughly defined my brand and the image I wanted to exude;

2) I developed my deliverables—the services I would deliver and the value-adds that clients would receive from me that they may not get from another similarly situated attorney; and

3) I honed in on my base, that is, the group comprised of my ideal clients.

You've read a bit about branding, defining your voice, and developing your deliverables in the preceding pages. By now, those parts should seem easy. After all, they're the same things that you would be doing in any industry whether you started a roofing company or a dental office. So what's left is honing in on your base. That means finding those clients (or, at least, finding where to find them) that, in a perfect world you would work with on every single case you took for the next thirty years. But, simply finding those clients isn't enough. Of course, for them to serve any real purpose for your business you need to convince them to work with you. Honing in on your base not only means finding clients that could be a good fit, it means figuring out how to make the sale.

The chances are good that how you define your ideal client is not all that different from how most of your competitors define their ideal clients. Take me, for example. As an estate planning attorney, there's a high likelihood that the middle-aged couple with a $3-5 million estate is the same ideal target client of dozens of other law firms in my geographic area. So, while that may be my ideal client, it's a steep uphill climb towards ultimately capturing that base over other more established practitioners and firms built on decades of quality service.

So, as a newly-minted attorney, how do you level the playing field?

The answer is by targeting clients that may currently fall on the fringe, or even outside of your target demographic, but that will grow their way into your ideal target group. For transactional attorneys, that concept is pretty easily illustrated regardless of the field in which you practice. For litigation firms, I think it works just as well. A personal injury attorney can easily target a very specialized subset of clients regardless of potential damages awards and spin that into experience and a reputation that is more likely to bring in a wide range of higher profile cases down the road.

How you incorporate that concept into your practice will depend on how and what you practice, but by thinking about ways to target clients on the fringes of what other firms commonly target, you increase your chances of building something successful.

Think about corporate law and picture a newly minted corporate attorney focusing primarily on transactional work like contracts, lease negotiations, mergers and acquisitions, and so on. An ideal client would likely be one with significant and consistent annual revenues (for obvious reasons). But, those companies typically have long-standing relationships with their outside counsel developed through years of collaboration. Well, whether it was one hundred years ago or two years ago, remember that those companies all started from the same place.

Targeting new businesses may not yield the same short-term return that working with established behemoths will, but it's certainly more easily accomplished. Generation X'ers and Millennials, fueled by today's technological culture, are consistently coming up with new and better ways to do things. And, they need lawyers to make sure they're doing them correctly. Look no further than the rapid rise of companies like Uber and Snapchat for illustrative tails of businesses that started with a simple idea and saw explosive growth, practically overnight. Imagine working with Travis Kalanick (Uber) or Evan Spiegel (Snapchat) before their rises. While never guaranteed, when you do quality work those clients are more inclined to bring you along for the ride.

Understandably, there's trepidation on the part of new attorneys to get involved with clients who have few assets other than visions of what they want their companies to be. New ideas are a dime a dozen and everyone naturally thinks they have the next big one. But, one of the threads of commonality running through the personalities of the successful entrepreneurs I've worked with over the years is a tremendous passion for their ideas. They all have a "do whatever it takes" mentality when it comes to presenting their ideas to the world. So, while yes, it's always a risk to deeply entwine yourself with a young business, you can hedge against that risk by targeting passionate people.

When you target passionate people, you're targeting individuals that have the drive to turn their grand ideas into sustainable operations. Your chances of taking on a young client that will grow into something great are enhanced. And, best of all, the likelihood that client will stay with you is pretty darn good, because you'll have an intimate knowledge of the business, its successes, and its struggles beyond anything that any outsider could acquire.

Targeting passionate people on the fringe of your target demographic is what can give you a leg up over your competition. While everyone else is out there competing for the same group of potential clients, you can have your pick of a different group of potential clients that is on their way to becoming the ideal client you've defined for your firm.

In the words of famed epigram author Ashleigh Brilliant,

> "Good ideas are common – what's uncommon are people who'll work hard enough to bring them about."

If you can find the ones that will you'll be well on your way to long-term success.

Don't Be Afraid to Fail

Earlier you read about developing a Plan B and thinking through what you'll do if things just don't work out in the solo game. Hopefully, you put some thought into it. And, hopefully you came to the realization that even if the absolute worst case scenario happens, the sun will still rise, and you'll still have the tremendous breadth of skill and knowledge that you have acquired through twenty-plus years of school and an unmeasurable number of valuable life experiences. The knowledge you acquired through your trial-by-fire solo gig will just be frosting on the cake.

The bottom line is that in the grand scheme of things, throwing in the towel as a solo practitioner is nothing more than a speed bump. It doesn't mean that you're a failure, and it certainly is not a measure of your self-worth. It simply means that the seemingly endless number of circumstances necessary for your ultimate success weren't all quite there.

Thinking about failure when we contemplate a new challenge is human nature. Frankly, if thoughts of the worst case scenario don't cross your mind when you think about the path your new business could take, you probably haven't thought all that much about what you even hope your firm becomes.

The problem with worse case scenarios, though, isn't that we contemplate them in the first place, because thinking about what can go wrong naturally prepares us for how to make it go right. The problem is that we usually think about them the wrong way.

When we think about everything that can go wrong, we each have a tendency to paint an inflated picture of what the consequences will be. All too often that inflated view of impending gloom leads us to reign in the risks we are willing to take, even at the expense of abandoning our ultimate objectives.

We rarely take the time reconsider the forgone conclusion that a worst case scenario we've projected in our mind is a likely, or even a possible outcome given our current knowledge of a situation.

Try thinking about a time when you've fallen into the trap of thinking that an outcome carried more significant consequences than it did. Whether it was asking out a stranger in a bar, giving a speech in front of a large group of people, or taking an important test I'm guessing the outcome was not even remotely close to the worst case scenario you imagined. Why?

Because worst case scenarios aren't logical.

If we take the time to step back and assess the perfect storm of events that would be necessary to bring about a worst-case outcome, we realize that the chances of it coming to fruition are minuscule.

Think about the challenge of starting a new business. Starting a new company means sacrificing a great deal, not only in your career but with your relationships, finances, and practically every other aspect of your life. It means taking a substantial risk in hopes of creating an ideal future. Thinking about failure is only natural because it means that you haven't yet given yourself that ideal future.

Entrepreneurs face many of the same fears. Whether it's a fear of not making enough money, developing a product that people don't need or want, fear of being sued, being viewed as incompetent, or something else, often, the object of the fear is the collective byproduct of multiple minor apprehensions. By breaking down an ultimate fear into those minor apprehensions, challenges become much less consequential.

For example, take a common fear amongst entrepreneurs in any industry: Fear of not making enough money to support oneself. No doubt, the consequences of that reality seem terrifying because making a living is the ultimate reason we work in the first place. But, there's so much more to that ultimate fear than just not making a living. Fear of not being a successful boss for yourself, fear of having to work for someone else, fear of adjusting your lifestyle to fit your new income, and fear that others will view you as a failure are all concerns that are inherent in the ultimate fear of not making a sufficient living financially. By walking the fear back into its more minor apprehensions, it becomes easier to articulate solutions should those fears become reality. All of a sudden the ultimate fear doesn't seem as overwhelming.

What if you're afraid of not making enough money to support yourself and your family? OK. So what would happen then? Well, you could take on a second part-time job doing something fun and engaging to cover some of the difference. While no doubt mind-numbingly boring, you could take on a few short-term document review projects. You could find another firm for which to do contract work. You could take court appointments. You could adjust your standard of living. As an absolute last resort, you could decide that working for someone else full time may be the best short-term move for you.

Put simply, your worst case scenario is doing the exact same thing you're doing now, except doing it for someone else. Ideal? No, especially considering that you really want to be your own boss. Sufficient to alleviate your fear? Absolutely.

What about others viewing you as a failure? Well, I'd guess they didn't even have the courage to put themselves out there and start their own firms. In fact, I'd bet that regardless of the size of your income or client base, your peers are going to view what you are doing with envy. Most attorneys don't have the courage to go out on their own and you've done it. That's something to be admired.

From the outset I would encourage you to articulate your ultimate fears and then break them down into the minor apprehensions inherent in them. Doing so will help you come to the realization that worst case scenarios aren't so bad. Approaching every day armed with that knowledge will free you to take the risks necessary to grown your business into what you ultimately want it to be.

Cross-Sell

Cross-selling is generally defined as selling a complementary product to an existing customer. Essential to increasing profits for any business, in the traditional sense, it should be easy to see why cross-selling should be a primary objective of any law firm, whether a solo operation or one with hundreds of attorneys.

But as a solo, I tend to think about cross-selling in another way. Along with focusing on cross selling your services, concentrate on cross-selling yourself.

Reflect on the traits that make you who you are as a lawyer and what makes your firm stand out from the competition. Building a book of business out of the gate requires you to draw upon every trait that a potential new client would find desirable. Are you relatable? Are you a good listener? Are you articulate? Are you like me, where your age alone makes you different from the vast majority of attorneys in your field of practice?

Imagine yourself getting ready to build a tree fort in your backyard (because, let's face it, you would still love to have a tree fort in your backyard). You've picked out the perfect tree for your fort, purchased the wood, unloaded everything, and laid out your supplies. You've even drawn up some sketches so you know how your finished product will look. You're ready to build, so you grab your tool box out of the garage, set it down, and open it up.

The first step in building your fort is to cut the wood that will form the frame. You lay out a long 2x4, grab a wrench out of your tool box, and lay it down next to your 2x4 so that you can make sure to make a precise measurement of the amount of wood you'll need to cut off. After marking a line where you will cut the wood, you reach into your tool box, grab your hammer, and begin smashing away at the piece of lumber in a vain attempt to make the cut.

The scenario above obviously sounds wrong. Of course, you wouldn't use a wrench to make precise measurements or a hammer to saw through a beam.

Selling yourself as an attorney that potential clients should hire is just like building that fort, and you are the tool box. It's one thing to know what you have in your toolbox, but it's another thing to know how to use those tools to achieve the desired result.

You need to know which instruments are appropriate for the job in the right situation. Potential clients are all different. From general characteristics, like having a legal issue in a general practice area, to the more specific, like personality traits and communication style, each potential client is going to be more receptive to certain traits that you possess than others. Knowing how to rely on the right ones at the right time is essential to building the trust and rapport necessary to win each one's business.

That's what I mean when I say "cross-sell." Realize that the collective traits that make you unique as an individual, an attorney, and a business owner run across an incredibly broad spectrum. Figuring out where that spectrum overlaps with a potential client's desires is essential to acquiring their business. What works for one may not work for another. Knowing how to find the right tools to build a relationship with each unique potential client will lead to your success as a practitioner.

Know Your Place

One thing I quickly came to realize was that, while a prudent young solo attorney should constantly keep his eyes and ears open for new business opportunities, there are times and places where being on the lookout for those opportunities probably shouldn't involve active self-marketing.

When I was starting out on my own, I remember reading some articles from seemingly respected networking and sales professionals that encouraged entrepreneurs to use every social interaction as a networking opportunity. They would point out that wherever one goes, whether a holiday party or breakfast meeting with an organized networking group, a finely tuned elevator pitch would leave a much clearer impression than casual conversation.

Picture yourself walking up to the hors d'oeuvres table at a small, casual cocktail party organized by some friends. Next to you stands someone you haven't seen before, but judging by the invite list to the party he is probably friends with the same people as you. After exchanging pleasantries, you decide that reality aside, this new acquaintance is almost assuredly a prime addition to your referral network. It shouldn't matter that you know little more about him than the color of his shirt. I mean, he has to know people, right? So naturally, you wait for your cue. Then, like clockwork, he asks, "So, what do you do?"

Of course, you can't just respond, "I'm a lawyer," right? That won't leave a memorable impression, you think to yourself. Instead, you immediately begin to rattle off some convoluted narrative about how you get to wake up every day and help people, so on, and so forth. Then, like all of those networking articles taught you, you casually hand over your business card.

I will guarantee you that using that approach in the wrong setting will lead to that person ignoring you for the rest of the event. Why? Because a casual cocktail party isn't the place for an elevator speech.

The last thing most people want to think about at a friend's party is work. Reading the room may have led to a different approach—one where a casual introduction led to a more in depth conversation later on as the party progressed. But, by not following social protocol, you've failed to take advantage of that party as a means to expand your network.

The way you speak and interact with people, whether longtime friends and colleagues or new connections, should vary. And, it should vary not only based on who you are speaking with but based on the setting in which you are interacting with them.

You're going to act differently whether you're at a party hosted by an old college friend or a formal state bar networking event. But, that doesn't mean that you need to change your message.

Remember that the presentation is just as important as the content of your interactions. Think about major companies that, generally speaking, cast a wide net when it comes to targeting consumers in a wide range of demographics—companies like McDonalds, Pepsi, and Target. They can place ads anywhere from a billboard in the middle of Montana to Times Square. They air commercials on Fox News and MTV, during the middle of the night and on Super Bowl Sunday.

But, while the branding is constant the delivery varies depending on who they are targeting.

Assuming that you have taken the time to develop your brand, knowing how to switch gears between audiences enables you to most effectively communicate your core values in a language that will reach your current audience.

So while formal state bar events and your weekly networking group meetings may be appropriate settings for a traditional elevator pitch, casual talk at the hors d'oeuvres table may be a more productive way to create meaningful contact and develop new relationships that may potentially fuel your business in the future.

Know your place and assess what each new situation calls for.

Embrace the Competition

The practice of law is unique. Often your biggest competitor can be your greatest ally, sometimes without you even realizing it.

So, I say embrace the competition. Doing so can benefit your firm in three primary ways:

1) it can lead to new business;
2) it can prompt new ideas; and
3) it can result in goodwill.

First, embracing your competition can lead to direct opportunities to increase your bottom line through actual case work. Established firms, as I'm sure you know by now, often have more work than personnel necessary to efficiently and expeditiously conclude the plethora matters on their dockets.

Whether it's because of a conflict of interest with another client, limited attorney availability to take on a new case, or a matter that doesn't mesh particularly well with the firm's primary focus overflow work and short-term contract projects and plentiful in most markets. It's simply a matter of building the right relationships with the folks at competing firms responsible for referring that work to other attorneys. By actively seeking to establish relationships with those key personnel you can successfully create a means of increasing your bottom line when there are natural lulls in your business.

Second, embracing the competition can lead to new ideas. More so now than ever before, solo and small firms must get creative when trying to stand out in an increasingly crowded industry. Every attorney brings a unique perspective to the development of a brand. By examining what other firms are doing to stand out from the crowd, you can draw inspiration for your firm, increase the quality of your product, and strengthen your image.

Do you remember when Instagram was just gaining a footing as a social media app? At the time, other apps and websites like Facebook and Flickr held a virtual monopoly on social media photo sharing. Instagram was started in 2010, long after Facebook, Flickr, and Twitter had been established. So, it was undoubtedly entering a market saturated with already-popular social media platforms. Armed with the distinct realization that people were using social media to see what their friends and family were up to on a regular basis, Instagram differentiated itself from the competition in a big way by doing something slightly different. By introducing filters and easy-to-use editing tools, Instagram made the photo sharing itself the focus, rather than treating photo sharing as one piece of a social media profile. Instagram just took an already existing reality and made it more fun.

Instagram's founders didn't pass on an opportunity to create an app they enjoyed just because someone was already out there doing essentially the same thing. They took an idea that was already proven to be popular and made it better. Within two months, Instagram had over 1 million users, and two years later it was purchased by Facebook for $1 billion.[26]

You may not be sitting on an idea quite as big, but try to remember that your competition can offer you the same benefits as competitors offered to Instagram. Think about what yours do that is popular and successful and then think of ways you can do it better.

Third, embracing the competition provides a way for you to develop goodwill with your competitors. And, would you believe it? That leads right back to generating new business for your firm.

Developing meaningful relationships with other solos and small firm attorneys is one of the most useful ways to grow your client base. If you haven't already, you'll quickly find that not every prospective client is a good fit for your firm.

There will come a time that a potential client comes calling with an issue that's beyond your expertise or comfort level. Regardless, taking on that potential client can be a tempting proposition, especially for a new solo concerned with establishing a customer base.

But, dabbling in unknown areas of law is a dangerous game. You're asking for trouble if you get yourself involved in cases that deal with areas of law in which you may know little more than what you picked up in that first-year torts class. At best you'll likely end up with an unhappy client, and at worst you could be facing a malpractice claim or the dreaded state ethics board.

So, instead of risking your professional reputation, think about referring those cases to other attorneys who may be better suited to handle them. Sure, it's tough to pass on a potential paycheck, but doing so provides you with an opportunity to nurture a relationship with your competition. The next time a potential client approaches that attorney with a case that needs to be passed off, I guarantee you're going to be at the front of her mind.

Every Company Starts From the Same Place

Do you know what companies like Facebook, General Electric, Ford, and McDonalds have in common with the historic bakery in your home town, the family-owned delicatessen, and that unique new shop in your local mall selling homemade soaps and miscellaneous trinkets?

They all started from the same place.

Well, not literally the exact same place, but they all started from the same initial point, and they all started without the one thing which is essential to creating and sustaining a successful business.

Customers.

Henry Ford didn't just wake up one day and decide he was going to found one of the world's largest automobile makers. In fact, he developed his first vehicle in his home and started a couple of not-so-successful businesses to sell it before becoming involved with the auto behemoth we all know today. [27]

Almost everyone is familiar with Mark Zuckerberg's founding of Facebook on the Harvard campus (see 'You May Be a Small Fish, But It's a Small Pond').

Just like Ford and Zuckerberg, the friendly elderly couple that operates the local bakery in your hometown, or the quirky woman that runs the soap shop started with just an idea—an idea that took vision, hard work, dedication, and perseverance to grow into the companies you see today.

It takes hard work to build a business. Anyone that tells you otherwise is either a) lying or b) your mother (who is just trying to make you feel better).

Everything you do isn't going to be effective. You need to continually experiment with new ways of doing things, whether it's in the development of your product, marketing, or operations. Assess the success of your methods, refine what doesn't work or what could be made better, and reassess things until they're effective. Henry Ford didn't hit it big with the Detroit Motor Company. He continually improved on his ideas and how to most successfully and efficiently implement them until he eventually developed a product and a process that changed the world. [28]

I find that pausing to think about some of the most successful companies and learn about how they rose to their positions atop the modern corporate pantheon can be incredibly inspiring. Learning what led those enterprises to succeed while some of their competitors failed can be illuminating for your small business.

Ideas are simple. They don't have to be profound. And, what you'll find by examining other successful companies is that turning those ideas into something that changes the way people live in the world around them doesn't have to be complex.

There are countless examples of products and systems that are so interwoven in our way of life that they seem timeless- their origins lost to the ages. For example, the ice cream cone—a quintessential symbol of Americana—was "invented" at the 1904 World's Fair when pastry concessionaire Ernest A Hamwi provided some of his waffle-like pastries to the adjacent ice cream booth since it had run out of serving bowls.[29]

Retrospectively, the story of its origin seems so simple that it's a wonder the ice cream cone wasn't invented fifty times before then. Putting ideas into action doesn't have to be complex. By studying successful businesses, you can find inspiration for turning your own great ideas into successes.

For your law firm, maybe that means finding a more efficient way to communicate with your clients, or perhaps it's a way to deliver a service that has somehow been absent from the legal industry.

Success doesn't happen overnight, but remember that it didn't happen overnight for Mark Zuckerberg, or Henry Ford, or any of those local shop owners either. Draw inspiration from them and the countless other successful companies in existence today. By doing so, I have no doubt that you'll be able to grow your business into a success story that is one day looked upon for inspiration by other entrepreneurs just starting out with their ideas.

Part 7: Weathering the Storms

"Just when the caterpillar thought the world was ending, he turned into a butterfly."

— Taoist Proverb

Lean on Family

By this point it should come as no surprise that many people in your life are going to be skeptical of your decision to start your own business. They may feel that, as a highly educated and bright individual, you could have any job you want. They may worry that, by starting your own law firm, you're digging a hole when it comes to career advancement. For every nay-sayer that makes his skepticism known, there are probably ten people that don't share their opinions with you who no doubt share the sentiment that starting your own business isn't a smart career move.

But, here's the important thing to always remember: people are skeptical of what they don't know. The people that urge you to explore a more traditional career path haven't spent the time to really think about what's involved in starting a business. They may see it as a poor choice because the only context within which they have to view "*work*" is via a traditional career path. They may view a large salary and benefits as the paramount requirements for a fulfilling work life. They may see the opportunity to advance through the ranks in an established company as a measure of career success.

Not to knock those folks, but as you're well aware by this point on your journey, there's usually more to life. Listening to all of that noise can have a detrimental effect on your ability to remain mindful of the reasons that succeeding as your own boss is so important to you. The result of viewing everything you're trying to build with pessimism should be obvious. It's terrible for business. And, it's during those times of doubt that a support system becomes absolutely essential.

What I've found on my entrepreneurial journey is that the most supportive proponents of my career choices have been my wife, my parents and my siblings. Sure, I have some close friends and colleagues who are legitimately interested in my business and who are cheerleaders for my ultimate success. But, my closest family members are the ones that intimately know the struggles I have faced on my journey, the successes I've seen, and the hard work, investment, and sacrifice that has gone into building a business that I can call my own.

Those closest to you are the ones that are likely to have trust and confidence in the decisions you make for yourself. They are also the most likely to be intimately affected by your choice to take this path. Whether it's just emotional investment in your success or an actual reliance on it financially, your family wants to see you succeed, and including them in your journey will give you a support system for when times get tough.

So how do you ensure that support system is robust? Well, the best thing I started doing was talking with them about how things are going in the firm. I don't mean the standard "Things are great!" answer we've all probably defaulted to when asked about how business is coming along. I mean really talking to them.

If you're married or in a committed relationship, I think this particularly applies to your partner. I'm by no means any sort of relationship expert, but what I've found is that keeping my wife in the loop about how things are going, for good or bad, can help alleviate fears—whether her fears that things may be strained financially if the clients don't call, or my concerns that the ultimate success of my business somehow correlates with the success of our marriage.

When your closest allies intimately know the successes you've seen, challenges you've encountered, and vision you have for the future of your business, they are better equipped to offer support and encouragement when things get challenging.

Mentally conquering the overwhelmingly difficult task of succeeding as an entrepreneur is no doubt a tall order for anyone. Doing so alone is virtually impossible. So, find yourself a support system and lean on the people it's made up of. People want to see you reach your goals. One of the best decisions I made was letting them help me reach for mine.

Find a Release

Starting your own business is like nothing you've ever done before (unless you've already started another business, of course). Not only will it consume the majority of your time but it will probably begin to consume your thoughts as well.

Both logistically and mentally, starting a business is incredibly demanding.

When you are your own boss, there's no guarantee of a paycheck. But, I assure you that you'll never have a shortage of work. From accounting to branding; from marketing to product development, networking, process improvement, billing and taxes, countless tasks always need to be done. Whether you have the time or not they need to be done by you.

Talk about stress!

If you're anything like me (and I'm guessing we have some similarities if you're thinking about striking out on your own as an attorney), then you often times find yourself worrying about the smallest details in everything you do. To an extent you're a perfectionist.

While that mentality and drive to strive for perfection can lead to tremendous success, it's always accompanied by the risk that you'll burn out.

And, when you're the sole person responsible for every little task and operation, it's easy to allow your work to have a detrimental effect on your psychological wellbeing.

That's why it's imperative that you find a release.

Finding a way to detach from your work is a good thing when you work for someone else, but it's a necessity when you work for yourself.

I have a number of friends that have highly successful careers complete with the substantial salaries and benefits that you might expect. I've thought to myself on countless occasions how it must be wonderful to have one of those paychecks. But, when I step back and think about the long hours they put in at the office, the travel, and the sacrifice, it always makes me wonder what the point is if they don't have the time to actually enjoy their monetary profusion. They may not have the choice to say no in their careers, but you do.

Never forget that you're starting a practice to create a better life for yourself. What good is all the sacrifice if you don't take the time to actually try to enjoy that life?

Now, enjoying life when there are so many constant stresses may not always be easy to do. So, it's essential that you find ways to separate yourself from the constant pressure to succeed and anxiety that sets in when things aren't going exactly as you had planned. Figure out what works for you and make time to do it. For me, that meant picking up running.

Running was something I always did but more so in the, "hey let's go do a light one-mile jog and pretend that we got a good workout" sense, and not in the, "go spend an hour really exerting myself at a high level" sense.

But when I started my firm, I began appreciating it as an activity which allowed me to mentally detach from the incredible pressure I put myself under every day. Whether it was at lunch or after a stressful phone call with a client, I began using running as a way to detach and clear my head. The alternative was to push forward with my work while my mind was somewhere else. And, if you've ever tried to do something important when something stressful was consuming you, then you know how unproductive, and frankly detrimental it can be.

Everything you do for your young business needs to be done with 100% focus. A half-assed effort is only going to lead to a half-assed outcome. When you're trying to build something that stands out from the crowd, half-assed results are quickly going to bury you and your business.

So, find a way to remove yourself and reset your focus. Whether it's painting, knitting, reading fiction or picking up photography, find something that you love and go do it. Don't be afraid to go do it in the middle of your work day if that's what it takes to step back and recharge your batteries. Sometimes that's the most productive thing you can do to move your business forward.

You Are Your Worst Enemy

I'll be the first to say that you should set some very high standards for what you want your firm to stand for and who you want to be as an attorney. More so, you should definitely set long-term goals for what you want your firm to become. But, doing so comes with inherent risk. An obvious consequence of striving to reach extremely lofty goals is that you may stumble along the way.

I can't count the number of times that things have been going along wonderfully in my business—income is flowing, clients are paying their bills on time, new leads are reaching out frequently—and then just like that, it stops.

The phone stops ringing, expenses begin to pile up, and at times it seems the current clients I'm working with have all gone radio-silent.

No matter how many times it happens it's always a challenge to tell myself that things haven't necessarily taken a turn because of anything I've done (or perhaps more accurately haven't done). I can tell myself over and over again that it's just the nature of the game, that especially when a business is young and still finding a footing, things move in cycles. It's one thing to tell yourself that, but it's another thing to believe it.

There are going to be times when your phone stops ringing or when you're waiting for your clients to provide feedback on some draft documents you previously sent to them so that you can continue working on their cases. There will be times when moving the business forward is simply outside of your control. Those times can be incredibly frustrating and mentally straining.

If you don't recognize them coming and have a plan to attack them when they arrive, you're going to begin to question whether you've actually done everything you can to make your business successful.

So, instead of waiting for those times to come—because I promise you they will—figure out how you're going to tackle them when they do.

How do you do that? Well, simply put, however works for you. Develop a plan that helps you step back from all of the fear and doubt and view the situation realistically.

My plan goes something like this:

1. Identify negative self-talk.

My first step is to tell myself that I need to differentiate between the times when things are actually going poorly and the times when things are just following the natural flow of a young business. When things are following a natural flow, like my weeks where things all of a sudden go silent, it's important to take all of the fear and self-doubt and view it realistically.

2. Re-characterize.

Secondly, I ask myself, "Are things really going poorly? Is there something I suddenly started doing differently that directly related to business stagnating?"

If the answer is yes, then it's pretty easy to identify the problem and develop some solutions.

But, if the answer is no, I stop telling myself it's something I did that caused the lull. I tell myself that it's not a reflection of me as an attorney or business owner. Every company, from your friendly neighborhood dry-cleaners to Microsoft, has its ups and downs. Maintaining that mentality goes a long way towards keeping a positive outlook on the future.

3. Make setbacks impersonal, temporary and specific.

The skies will clear and things will pick up again. There are few things in this book I'm more confident in than that. Why? Because it's happened to me time and time again.

So the third thing I do is I disconnect from setbacks. It's important to keep in mind that there are peaks and valleys in the journey of growing a business. They all have to be traversed. Building a law firm from the ground up is about the voyage, not the immediate outcomes. Believe in yourself and stay focused on your long-term goals, and you'll get the results you're aiming for.

It's OK Not Knowing

Comprehensive statistics on law firm success rates are tough to come by. But, what is certain is that every year, a substantial chunk of young firms fail. Wondering if yours will be one of them is probably one of the most common thoughts you have at this point.

Worrying about how much you'll make in year three or year ten if your firm is still around is a dangerous game. There are just too many unknowns.

I remember a lunch meeting I had with a good friend from childhood a few years after starting my practice. I was still in the building stage and continually performing the mental gymnastics that come with starting anything new. I repeatedly questioned everything I was doing and whether the choices I was making were the right ones.

My friend, from the web marketing and design field, had done work for numerous companies for years after graduation with plenty of success stories to share. But, eventually he came to a point where he decided to head out on his own.

As he was sharing his story, it became evident that there came a time where the same light bulb lit up for him as it did for me. He came to a point in his career where he suddenly didn't feel like he was finding satisfaction with the monotony of his work.

He shared in detail the circumstances that led to his decision to leave corporate America and start his own company. Needless to say, it wasn't a fair situation, but it was one that took tremendous courage to exit. He shared the details of the day he decided that he wanted something different and something more fulfilling out of his career. Once he decided he wanted something else, leaving was easy.

While his expertise is in a completely different industry than mine, the fears are the same. Leaving a secure job with benefits and a steady paycheck is a terrifying move. Striking out on your own with nothing behind you but your confidence and what little reputation you may have for excellence in a profession is similarly intimidating.

As we continued talking, he shared with me how he still worried about where clients would come from (even though he was doing much better than he wanted to admit to himself). He told me a story about a trying time about a year and a half after he started the business when, during a two-month span, he lost three clients and a substantial portion of the company's income. He spent weeks sitting in his office trying to figure out where he went wrong with those customers and what he could have done to keep them. He was lost. He could feel doubt creep in about whether leaving his comfortable job at his previous company was worth the stress of not knowing how the next month's bills were going to get paid.

But what he said next struck me. And it struck me in a way that, strangely, gave me a belief that what I was doing was going to be successful.

He said, "Mike, this is business. I didn't know why those clients left, but it happens. Once I realized that I did everything I could to serve their needs, and they left regardless, I was able to tell myself that clients are going to leave sometimes, not because of anything I do or don't do, but just because that's business."

That realization helped remove the tremendous burden of worry from his shoulders and let him focus on building his business. Sure, he didn't know how he was going to replace that income (he did, by the way, with plenty of new business over the next few months), but he knew he had time to figure out ways to make the business work. He sat down with his newly found free time and focused on his marketing efforts and defining his product. He thought about what made his firm different and better than every other Chicago web-based marketing firm, honed in on those differences, and used that new clarity to move his business forward.

When he lost those clients, he didn't know which way the business was going to go, and he was scared. But, what he realized, and what you need to understand as a new business owner, is that there are going to be moments where all of a sudden the success you were building comes to a screeching halt. Positively reacting to those moments is going to be critical to moving your business forward.

The first time it happens, it's going to be terrifying, and you're probably not going to know how to overcome it right away. But that's OK. Take a breath and remember that the situation isn't personal. *It's business.*

Only then can you effectively think about what you're going to do about it. You can mope about why things went wrong, or as my friend did, you can use the situation to figure out how you can be even better at what you do.

You may not know what that looks like, but it's OK not knowing. Just keep moving.

You're Going to Be Wrong

Deciding to take the plunge into the world of business is like jumping off a cliff into a river. Standing on the top of that cliff, you can look out over the entire body of water and see obstacles like large stones or branches that you'll naturally want to avoid. You can examine the shoreline and determine the point where the water looks deep enough to plunge safely below the surface without too much concern for hitting the bottom. You can get a fairly complete picture of what you're about to do and where you hope to land.

So you jump.

After a few seconds of unsure anticipation, you splash through the surface of the water. But, something's wrong. After half a second, your feet slam into the river bed.

As it turns out, the sediment floating in the water made the bottom hard to see. From up on top of the cliff, the water looked deceptively deep, when in reality it was much shallower. The projections you made before leaping into a freefall were inaccurate, obscured by the conditions below the surface which you weren't able to see or account for since you had never jumped off this particular cliff into this particular river before.

Luckily, the riverbed is soft enough that you escape with only a sprained ankle. But, lesson learned. No matter what it looks like on the surface, there are always going to be unknowns below. Sometimes you're going to make educated decisions based on what you can see. But at times, things may not work out perfectly, and you could walk away with a sprained ankle.

No matter how much you prepare or how much you try to predict what the future holds, there are times that you're going to be wrong.

Starting a business is like jumping off that cliff into the river below. All the plans, projections, and predictions in the world can't account for unknown variables below the surface. If they could, then starting a business would be simple and everyone would be doing it.

It's often said that failure is the biggest key to success in business. I don't buy that. Sure, learning from failure is invaluable, but I think it's nonsensical that you need to fail at business before succeeding like it's some rite of passage. So, I think going into your new business venture, it's important to block out all the naysayers that are going to tell you to embrace failure as some key to success.

At the same time, I think it's important to accept that everything is not going to go perfectly. You're not going to do everything right the first time.

The chances are good that you'll make the inevitable rookie mistakes of putting your advertising dollars in the wrong place or failing to close the sale after a seemingly successful meeting with a potential client. But, it's been my experience that it's also really hard to make a catastrophic error that can derail your entire business. As a lawyer, follow the rules of professional responsibility and you're probably going to make it out OK.

When you do hit a roadblock, take a minute, step back from the problem, learn why it went wrong, and figure out how to improve it. Then, move on.

I remind myself of that objective with a sticky note I keep on the monitor in my office. It says,

"Make setbacks impersonal, temporary, and specific."

You're going to be wrong sometimes. But, when setbacks happen; when you make mistakes, it's imperative to keep them in perspective. Very rarely are they an ultimatum on you or your skills as an entrepreneur or attorney, so don't overblow them. They're punches that didn't go your way. They're that shallow water with the soft sediment. So, when faced with them, climb up, dry yourself off, and move on.

You're Also Going to Be Right

While you're going to make mistakes, they are going to be overshadowed by the plethora things you do right.

One of the biggest challenges of going solo is developing confidence in the business and legal decisions you make. When you work for someone else, or even as part of a collaborative team, it's easy to develop a sense of safety in your decision-making because there are other people around to bail you out if something goes wrong.

But, when you work for yourself you don't have that luxury. Every decision, whether wildly successful or terribly unsuccessful, carries consequences that directly impact your business and your reputation. That can be an intimidating prospect to face.

The fact of the matter is that it comes with the territory. There's no way around it if you want to strive as a business owner and as a solo attorney. That's the bad news if you're used to having memos proofread and decisions made by supervisors or more senior attorneys.

The good news is that your decisions are going to be right a hell of a lot of the time. Why? Well, first, because you're probably an incredibly intelligent and organized individual. After all, you did complete (or are in the process of completing) law school. But second, you're going to be right more than you realize, because of a simpler reason: this is your business, and you get to dictate the path it follows.

Making decisions that further the goals and aspirations you have for your company—which you know intimately—is much easier than deciding what's best for someone else's business.

With your firm, you are aware of every precise detail about how it functions, from budget figures memorized down to the dollar to client acquisition strategies and what makes your brand unique. That's because those aren't things that you've been taught. They're things that you feel. They are internalized to such an extent that the standards you have set for yourself are not just goals articulated in a business plan. They are a part of you.

When you sit down and really think about what your business stands for and how it's going to become what you want it to be, you will realize that the decisions you make to push it towards those aspirations are not static, and they are not isolated from every other decision you make for the company.

In doing so, you will begin to act not only with your head but with your heart. You'll start to make decisions based on feelings. And quickly, you'll realize that you are no longer second guessing the decisions you make because they are flowing organically from your vision for your company's future.

When you internalize your decision-making and make it a process rather than making each decision a separate task with an isolated result, the fear of being wrong will disappear.

So, have confidence in the decisions you make and realize that you're going to end up being right much more than you're going to end up being wrong.

Part 8: Define Success

"Success is liking yourself, liking what you do, and liking how you do it."

— Maya Angelou

Focus on the Long Term by Conquering the Short Term

Everyone is familiar with the story of the tortoise and the hare and its lessons of patience, persistence, and the value of incremental planning. As we all know, the tortoise was successful because he had a plan and he kept moving. While the hare was focused on the eventual result—winning the race—the tortoise was just focused on taking the next few steps towards the finish line.

When you're running your own business, especially in the early days, it's essential to remember that you're in it for the long haul. If success came overnight, everyone would work for themselves. But, success doesn't come easy, and it certainly doesn't come quickly.

Building a great business is about taking thousands of baby steps towards your ultimate goal. Whether you decide that success is defined by a paycheck of a certain size, helping clients of a particular type, or just freeing yourself from the grips of your career and achieving a better work-life balance, you're never going to reach that goal without taking thousands of individual steps along the way.

I remember the first month after I decided that I was going to be my own boss and committed to building my firm full-time. There was plenty of excitement as I faced new challenges every day, but there was also a tremendous amount of fear. I wasn't afraid of failing, necessarily. But, I was scared of not knowing how I was going to succeed. I was afraid that I wasn't working hard enough, fast enough, or efficiently enough because when I thought about where I wanted to be as an attorney and a business owner, it was simply overwhelming how far away I was from my vision.

In retrospect, it's almost embarrassing to say, but it honestly took me some time to figure out that I wasn't going to reach the point at which I could say that my vision for the firm had come to fruition easily or quickly. I sternly believed that in six months, maybe a year at the most, I was going to have a steady stream of clients and income equivalent to what I would be earning working for someone else. That didn't happen for me. Based on my first-hand experience and numerous discussions with other solos, that's not a realistic expectation and probably isn't going to happen for you either.

Failure to realize instant success can be frustrating. But, it's far more frustrating hearing that others in your same position were seemingly able to build their firms into highly successful operations instantaneously. Talk to a few other solos at a networking event or conference and you'll quickly begin to feel like you must be doing something wrong. After all, you seem to be the only solo on the planet that took longer than six months to begin to see some measurable success in your business.

But, here's the thing: no one likes to admit that things aren't going as great as they seem to be going from the outside. We're all familiar with the tremendous pressure to be successful in our profession, and that doesn't just magically go away when you start your own firm (frankly, it probably gets much worse, at least in the beginning). Giving off the impression that one is successful is an obvious way to deflect all that pressure from the outside. And, when you're not successful but people expect you to be, what do you do? You lie about your success.

You're going to come across dozens of other attorneys that will insist that they are twice as well off as their peers working for established firms. They'll explain that it was a little tough getting started, but after a few months things stabilized, and now they're looking to hire a few associates because they're so busy.

Sure, some new solos see success come along at warp speed, but nine times out of ten, what most others tell you is not going to be anything even close to the truth. Those other solos are struggling to get a foothold just like you. And, to diffuse the pressure to succeed being applied by outside forces, they fudge the truth. The problem is that, in doing so, they are just creating more pressure to meet the false narrative they've fabricated for themselves. Doing so leads to panic, and panic leads to carelessness. The risk of being dishonest with yourself about the state of your business is that you lose sight of where you are on the journey.

Once I allowed myself to see the value in focusing on the journey and breaking down my long-term goals into achievable and measurable short-term objectives, I was able to create a plan consisting of articulable steps which would lead me to my ultimate ideas of success.

So now I'm honest with myself and honest with others. When someone asks how things are going, I tell them. If that means I just had my best month ever, great. If it means business has been slow, that's OK. People aren't nearly as judgmental about your firm and how it's doing as you are.

When I started being honest about things, a funny thing happened. I found that other solos were honest about the state of their firms too. By removing the often-imaginary outside pressure to succeed, you will eliminate the pressure to reach quick results, and you'll be able to focus on building the business in a sustainable way. It's going to help you realize that the steps you're taking to develop your company are the right ones to take. You will find that the point on your journey at which you may be on puts you right on track.

By placing your focus on short-term goals, you give yourself the ability to create a plan. Instead of aimlessly working in the hope of eventually building a great company, breaking the mountain down into molehills gives you structure and forces you to focus on the task at hand. It forces you to strive for perfection in everything you do—whether it's creating a new process around communicating with potential clients or analyzing your expenses and how to trim your costs. It allows you to do so on your own terms and not just because the outside world may demand it. It is in striving for perfection in each of those small steps and short-term goals that you are going to create a successful business.

A great company is made up of thousands of parts. Figuring out what those parts are and how they fit together will make you successful.

Focus on Process Not Outcomes

When you're in the process of incrementally building something substantial it can be challenging to step back and envision the ultimate goal. Think about the laborers who built the Pyramids of Giza. I assume that the ancient Egyptians hauling massive stones across the sand weren't exactly focused on how each block fit into the final architectural masterpiece. Instead, their goal (presumably besides not dying) was simply to add another stone to the massive structure they were enlisted to build. I can't imagine that their focus was on anything other than the immediate task at hand because the Great Pyramid alone is made up of over 2.3 million limestone blocks weighing in at an average of 2.5 tons each! It must have been unconscionable even to imagine the size and grandeur of the final structure.

By most accounts, the Egyptians developed state of the art systems for transporting the limestone blocks from quarries, up the Nile, and over to the construction site. Once there, the massive stones were unloaded from boats and moved by oxen and men across the sand on a constructed slipway coated in oil, a process which drastically reduced friction between the sand and the blocks and made moving the stones much easier (relatively speaking, of course). That process enabled the ancient Egyptians to accomplish an awe-inspiring feat—one that may not have been possible without a focus on improving the simple process of moving stones. `

If I were building one of the pyramids, I think that the mere thought alone of hauling a two-and-a-half ton block across a hot desert would make me want to give up. But, for the ancient laborers, that task was a necessity. So, instead of focusing on the immense challenge of hauling millions of those blocks into position, every day, for the next twenty years, the focus was on making the monumental, repetitive task more efficient.

In that regard, building your law firm is like the ancients building the pyramids. Keeping a focus on short term success and perfecting your business brick by brick can be challenging when all you want to see is big-picture results.

Believe me, when I say that it's far too easy to fall into the trap of looking at what you haven't done instead of all of the things you have done to make your business great.

There will probably be times when you aren't pulling in enough money or aren't attracting the type of clients you want as often as you'd like. You may be down on yourself because things simply aren't where you want them to be. But, when that happens, remember the example of the ancient Egyptians. I can't fathom a way that those laborers were remotely concerned about what the pyramids were going to look like when complete. Their focus was on improving the process so that they could make the objective more attainable.

When you find yourself thinking too far ahead, shift your focus onto the building blocks that will enable you to reach those distant results rather than the results themselves.

Instead of giving up because things aren't where you want them to be, figure out what you can do in the short term to improve on the things you have control over. If the issue is client acquisition, revisit your business plan and hone your processes. Work on articulating who your perfect client is and developing your acquisition strategy for that customer. Narrow your focus and perfect how you'll get one client before worrying about how you'll get dozens more.

Maybe client matters are taking too long to close and it's affecting cash flow. What can you do? Well, you can take a look at your processes. Are you doing the same thing for each client? Are there certain common issues that bog things down? Is your workflow automated in a way that customers are being reminded to keep things moving? Focus on the processes that will lead to consistent results. Eventually, those results will come, and you will begin to see your ideal firm take shape.

In the words of tennis great Arthur Ashe,

"Success is a journey, not a destination. The doing is often more important than the outcome."

Reclassify Compensation

There is always going to be someone with a nicer apartment, a better car, a bigger paycheck, and a more prestigious professional title. And, I don't mean just anyone. I'm talking about your friends.

If you're starting your own law firm I would guess that, while you still think those things would be nice to have, your idea of success may be different than that of your peers. If you're like me, you started (or are thinking about starting) a firm for many reasons. Whether you wanted more balance between work and leisure time, more time with your family, or simply an opportunity to challenge yourself and build something that you can stand behind, you may have very different priorities than your peers.

While all of us at sometime or another have felt envious of someone's generous paycheck, luxurious new car, or lofty professional title, it might be surprising to hear that it's a two-way street. Trust me. I promise you that owning your own firm will often make you the object of others' envy too. Your friends are going to envy that you have the flexibility to work with who you want to work with and that you, and you alone, are in charge of the growth of your firm. They'll admire you for your courage—courage that was imperative to setting out on your own without a financial safety net—and your ability to persevere when times get tough.

Will you have the sleek car and fat paycheck? Hopefully, in time. But, if those are the primary reasons you started your own firm, then solo life may not be for you, at least not at this stage in your career.

It's one thing for me to tell you that there are plenty of envious characteristics inherent in one who operates his own business, but in reality, actually focusing on those freedoms instead of the paycheck or prestige is easier said than done.

I remember when I decided to take the plunge and open my firm. I spent countless hours worrying about whether my salary was going to be big enough to permit me to live the way I wanted to live. I worried that I wouldn't be able to grow the firm into something sustainable, and more importantly, something of which I could be proud. I thought about all the other attorneys I knew—the ones that worked in the larger firms in the city collecting six-figure paychecks in the first few years out of law school. Many times, I caught myself envying what they had: the prestige, the beautiful office, and the premium compensation package. There was a big part of me that wanted those things.

But, then I would remind myself that they get into those nice offices at 7:00AM and don't leave until late in the evening. They work Saturdays. They may need to back out of personal commitments if big cases come along. Sure, they're employed at firms with prestigious names and long track records of success, but the work many of them do is dictated by some partner who may care more about case management fees than actually developing a collaborative working relationship with his associates. They have the big salaries, but little time to enjoy spending them.

Of course, I love my friends in those positions dearly, and they are doing what makes them happy professionally. But, that doesn't mean it's what I would want for myself. The more I thought about all the things that society typically views as ideal in a career, the more I realized that the things we sometimes have to give up to get them are just as valuable and often much more fulfilling.

Can you acquire all of the same benefits that those large firm lawyers enjoy? Absolutely. Through hard work, there's no doubt that you can reach that level of compensation or prestige in your practice area. But, being your own boss means that you'll be able to have all of those things (eventually) plus so much more.

Compensation as a solo attorney comes in other forms. Whether it's the freedom to watch all of your son's soccer games or pick your daughter up from school, you have the opportunity to choose how work fits into your life and not the other way around. You'll get to build your vacation time around your spouse's schedule without having to worry about getting bogged down with a last minute project. You'll have the freedom to grab lunch with an intriguing new connection on Thursday afternoon without having to worry about how many billable hours you'll need to make up by making such a commitment. Simply put, you'll have the freedom to build your business however you choose without sacrificing the things that are important to you (unless you make the conscious choice to do so).

Too often we think of compensation as a dollar figure. But, working for yourself means that you're free to enjoy very different kinds of rewards. Freedom, flexibility, the ability to apply yourself creatively and challenge yourself, and satisfaction knowing that every step forward your business takes is a direct result of your actions that you take are all rewarding outcomes inherent in a solo career.

So, reclassify compensation for yourself. The paycheck will come if you work hard enough. But, until it does, pay attention to the other intangible benefits that being your own boss brings.

Enjoy the Journey

Starting your own firm gives you the ability to dictate the terms of your professional life. Every day is an opportunity to make your life into what you want it to be. Every client you serve and every connection you build is an accomplishment. Each and every one of those small victories deserves to be celebrated.

In anything worth doing, there's something magical about the journey, and sometimes it's easy to forget that the journey can be just as rewarding as the goal. At times, we can get so wrapped up in the pursuit of a finite result that we forget to appreciate the present.

No doubt on occasion you've woken up on a Monday morning and immediately began counting down on the hours until Friday evening. We've all done it. In the words of esteemed 80's rock band Loverboy, "Everybody's working for the weekend." But, that mentality figuratively shortens our lives by over seventy percent. Living for the weekend –the light at the end of the tunnel—makes us miss everything happening around us on our ways there.

There is no grand conclusion to the process of building a law firm. Think about it. No matter how big the business gets, how many clients you help, or how much money you make, is there some finite point in the future at which you could say you've made it to the finish line? Probably not.

Chances are pretty good that you're not going to sell your firm or get acquired like some tech startup. If you like what you do, you'll keep doing it and keep finding ways to use your profession as a tool that enables you to improve your quality of life and the lives of those around you. And, if you don't like what you're doing, you'll find something else to do. Of course, if you already knew that there would come a time when you weren't satisfied as a solo, you probably wouldn't be starting your own firm right now.

Only time will tell what your firm will become, but you have the power to control its direction. Rewards are great, but I'd encourage you to sit back sometimes and try to enjoy this crazy journey that you're on because you're not going to get to go through it again.

In the words of Ferris Bueller,

"Life moves pretty fast. If you don't stop and look around once in a while, you could miss it."

About the Author

Michael Brennan (University of the Pacific, JD '10, University of Wisconsin-Madison, BA '07) is a solo practitioner currently residing in Illinois. He operates a virtual law office serving clients throughout Illinois, Minnesota and Wisconsin. His practice focuses on estate planning and legal issues commonly seen in the entrepreneurial and small business realm.

Michael started The Virtual Attorney with little more than a dream and a computer. He learned how to operate a law firm by simply doing it. He hopes that, by sharing his story and the lessons he learned along the way, he can provide others with the tools they need to realize they too can make their dreams of working for themselves a reality.

Notes and References

[1] At publication of this book, statistics for the classes of 2014 and 2015 were unclear, though signs point to growth increasing, albeit slowly.

[2] "Employment for the Class of 2013 - Selected Findings." *Employment for the Class of 2013 - Selected Findings* (2014). National Association of Legal Professionals, 2014. Web. Nov. 2015.

[3] *Report on the State of the Legal Market.* Rep. Center for the Study of the Legal Profession at Georgetown University Law Center and Thomson Reuters Peer Monitor, 9 Jan. 2015. Web. Nov. 2015.

[4] "Experience Avon's History." *History.* Web. 06 Feb. 2015.

[5] Avon Products, Inc. *Annual Report,* 2014 Web. 02 August 2015.

[6] American runner Ryan Hall bested Khannouchi's time at the 2011 Boston Marathon. However, that course is not eligible for official records due to a variety of factors.

[7] Mihoces, Gary; *Marathon's 26.2-mile run tests body, mind.* USA Today, USA Today. 20 Feb. 2003. Web. July 2015.

[8] Silkenat, James R., and Harvey B. Rubenstein. "Solo and Small-firm Lawyers: A Renewed Priority for Bar Associations." *Bar Leader* (Spring 2011). *American Bar Association.* American Bar Association, Spring 2013. Web. Summer 2015.

[9] As quoted in Louis Untermeyer. *Makers of the Modern World: The Lives of Ninety-two Writers, Artists, Scientists, Statesmen, Inventors, Philosophers, Composers, and Other Creators who Formed the Pattern of Our Century.* 1955.

[10] According to some, the distance is actually much longer.

[11] Shaw, Bernard. *Back to Methuselah, a Metabiological Pentateuch. Rev. Ed., with a Postscript.* New York &: Oxford UP, 1947. Print.

[12] Christensen, Clayton M. The Innovator's Dilemma: When New Technologies Cause Great Firms to Fail. Boston, Mass: Harvard Business School Press, 1997. Print.

[13] "Key Concepts." *Clayton Christensen.* Oct. 2012. Web. Summer 2015.

[14] For an enlightening read on color psychology, I recommend: Birren, Faber. *Color Psychology and Color Therapy; a Factual Study of the Influence of Color on Human Life.* New Hyde Park, NY: U, 1961. Print.

[15] GE famously attributed $350 million in saving to Six Sigma techniques utilized during 1998. That number eventually grew to over $1 billion. Dusharme, Dirk "*Six Sigma Survey: Breaking Through the Six Sigma Hype*", Quality Digest (August 2002).

[16] "Average Annual Hours Actually Worked per Worker." *Average Annual Hours Actually Worked per Worker*. Web. 06 Apr. 2016.

[17] *Id.*

[18] Adam, Hajo, and Adam D. Galinsky. "Enclothed Cognition." *Journal of Experimental Social Psychology* 48.4 (2012): 918-25. Web.

[19] *Id.*

[20] Hatch, Stephani L. et al. "The Continuing Benefits of Education: Adult Education and Midlife Cognitive Ability in the British 1946 Birth Cohort." *The Journals of Gerontology Series B: Psychological Sciences and Social Sciences* 62.6 (2007): S404–S414.

[21] Herman, Aguinas et al. "Benefits of Training and Development for Individuals and Teams, Organizations, and Society." *The Annual Review of Psychology* 2009.60.451-74.

[22] *Id.*

[23] *Id.*

[24] Phillips, Sarah. "A Brief History of Facebook." *The Guardian*. Guardian News and Media, 2007. Web. Apr. 2015.

[25] The creation and rise of Facebook is obviously a much more complex web of circumstances that what can be accurately detailed in the space of these pages. For a wonderfully detailed account of the history of Facebook, see Ben Mezrich's "The Accidental Billionaires: The Founding of Facebook: a Tale of Sex, Money, Genius and Betrayal." Anchor Books, 2010.

[26] Rusli, Evelyn M. "Facebook Buys Instagram for $1 Billion." *Dealbook*. The New York Times, 9 Apr. 2012. Web. Spring 2015.

[27] Ford built his first quadricycle in his home at 58 Bagley Avenue in Detroit, Michigan in 1896.

[28] Ford initially founded the Detroit Automobile Company with backing from lumber baron William H. Murphy; however the company dissolved shortly after its introduction. Ford then founded the Henry Ford Company with Murphy as a financial backer. Due to disagreements with personnel, Ford eventually left the company (which would later become Cadillac). Ford then began a new venture with financial backing from coal dealer Alexander Y. Malcomson and some other investors. That entity would grow into what is currently the Ford Motor Company. Bryan, Ford R. "The Birth of Ford Motor Company." *The Borth of Ford Motor Company*. Henry Ford Heritage Association. Web. Fall 2015.

[29] "The History of the Ice Cream Cone", *The History of the Ice Cream Cone*. International Dairy Foods Association. Web. 28 Dec. 2015.

Made in the USA
Middletown, DE
21 January 2018